"What a brilliant idea! We know that t[h]... stantly engaged in argument and contr[o]... the complacent, sometimes encouraging the despairing. So why not bring to life those who engaged with them, royalty and peasants, religious professionals and political conspirators. Disciplined imagination is a powerful tool in bringing the Scriptures to life and John Goldingay puts his well-informed imagination to work here in ways that entertain and educate in equal measure, both in the service of hearing the living voice of these spokesmen of the God of Israel."

—CHRISTOPHER J. H. WRIGHT, Langham Partnership

"Goldingay takes the often-overlooked Minor Prophets and brings clarity not only to their message but also to the tensions they provoked. Rather than making strawmen of the prophets' audience, Goldingay gives them caring hearts and persuasive causes. In so doing he helps us see the relevance of their messages for life today. A fabulous tool for intuitively engaging these less accessible biblical texts."

—SHANNON LAMB, InterVarsity Christian Fellowship USA

"Today we need to reintroduce people to the prophetic word. No one is more equipped to do that in a creative mode than John Goldingay! By presenting excerpts from the Twelve Prophets as responses to letters from citizens, officials, and religious leaders, he reminds us that these (uncomfortable) divine words were delivered within and for concrete settings. Timely, yet timeless as Scripture, these prophets continue to speak into real life to challenge God's people."

—M. DANIEL CARROLL R. (RODAS), Scripture Press Ministries Professor of
Biblical Studies and Pedagogy, Wheaton College and Graduate School

"John Goldingay's *The Lost Letters to the Twelve Prophets* are a sparkling exercise in disciplined imagination that opens up the Minor Prophets. Through these letters we are introduced to the issues and challenges faced as people worked out what it meant to be faithful in a changing world and how the prophets address them. Written with wit and insight into their world, they also show us how these prophets continue to speak into ours."

—DAVID G. FIRTH, Tutor in Old Testament and Academic Dean, Trinity College Bristol

THE LOST LETTERS TO THE
TWELVE PROPHETS

THE LOST LETTERS TO THE
TWELVE PROPHETS

IMAGINING THE
MINOR PROPHETS' WORLD

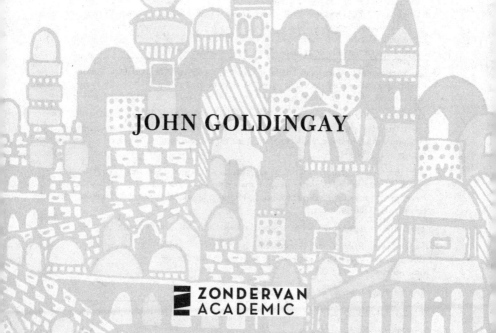

JOHN GOLDINGAY

ZONDERVAN
ACADEMIC

ZONDERVAN ACADEMIC

The Lost Letters to the Twelve Prophets
Copyright © 2022 by John Goldingay

Requests for information should be addressed to:
Zondervan, *3900 Sparks Dr. SE, Grand Rapids, Michigan 49546*

Zondervan titles may be purchased in bulk for educational, business, fundraising, or sales promotional use. For information, please email SpecialMarkets@Zondervan.com.

ISBN 978-0-310-14504-2 (audio)

Library of Congress Cataloging-in-Publication Data
Names: Goldingay, John, author.
Title: The lost letters to the Twelve Prophets : imagining the Minor
   Prophets' world / John Goldingay.
Description: Grand Rapids : Zondervan, 2022. | Includes index.
Identifiers: LCCN 2022009831 (print) | LCCN 2022009832 (ebook) | ISBN
   9780310125570 (paperback) | ISBN 9780310125587 (ebook)
Subjects: LCSH: Bible. Minor Prophets--Criticism, interpretation, etc. |
   Bible. Minor Prophets--Miscellanea.
Classification: LCC BS1560 .G648 2022 (print) | LCC BS1560 (ebook) | DDC
   224/.906--dc23/eng/20220317
LC record available at https://lccn.loc.gov/2022009831
LC ebook record available at https://lccn.loc.gov/2022009832

The author is represented by Pieter and Elria Kwant (trading as Piquant).

Cover design: Bruce Gore | Gore Studio, Inc.
Cover: © V. Kuntsman / Shutterstock; 123RF; Iconfinder.com
Interior design: Sara Colley

Printed in the United States of America

22 23 24 25 26 27 28 29 30   /TRM/   12 11 10 9 8 7 6 5 4 3 2 1

CONTENTS

PREFACE

What led the prophets to talk about the things that they do talk about? What were they responding to? If only we knew what the Israelites themselves were thinking and experiencing and doing! If we knew the questions people might be asking the prophet, their words might suddenly become clearer without our needing commentaries to clarify them.

There was once an illuminating book called *Epistles to the Apostle* by Colin Morris, in which he imagined letters that people in the church in Corinth (for instance) wrote to Paul, to which Paul was responding in documents such as First and Second Corinthians. The presupposition was indeed that it would be easier to understand Paul's replies when you knew what might have been the questions that were addressed to him. So suppose we do try to imagine the letters people wrote to some prophets, to which they were then responding?

Prophets did write and they did get written to. Jeremiah exchanged letters with exiles from Jerusalem in Babylon (see Jeremiah 29). So in this book I'm trying to imagine how people might have written to some of the prophets, and specifically, to the prophets whose names are at the top of the twelve shorter prophetic books at the end of the Old Testament—the First Testament, as I like to call it. Admittedly, many of the "letters" in this book involve communication between people who live in the same town, so don't take me too literally when I use the letter form.

The letters come from my imagination, working backwards from comments the prophets themselves make, or from other material in the First Testament, or from archaeological discoveries. Occasionally the writers are people we know about from elsewhere; my favorite is Ms. Makbiram, whose house in Hazor in Galilee I have visited. (There's nothing implausible about the idea of a woman like Ms. Makbiram in Israel's world taking an initiative in writing a letter; scribes and writers in the Middle East included women as well as men, so she could have written it herself, or she could have dictated it to someone.) Some of the other people in the letters are individuals the prophets refer to—people such as kings and priests. Sometimes I've given people names that appear in plausible contexts elsewhere in the First Testament. The way names work in the prophets compares with the way they used to work in Europe: people were most commonly known by their own name followed by their father's name, so that "Hosea ben Beeri" means "Hosea son of Beeri" and "Gomer bat Diblaim" means "Gomer daughter of Diblaim." Adding the father's name is like adding a surname. But people might be known by where they came from ("Micah of Moresheth") or by their trade ("Jonathan the scribe").

After the letters representing things people might have wanted to say to prophets, I give you the actual words of the prophets that could have been responses to such letters; the translation is mine, from *The First Testament: A New Translation* (InterVarsity) with modification to the spelling of names. After the quotes there are some notes to tell you more about the backdrop to the correspondence I have imagined. If you want to know more, I have said more in these commentaries:

Daniel and the Twelve Prophets for Everyone
(Louisville: Westminster John Knox, 2016)

Hosea to Micah (Grand Rapids: Baker Academic, 2020)
Minor Prophets II (with P. J. Scalise), for Nahum,
Habakkuk, Zephaniah, and Haggai (Grand Rapids:
Baker Books, 2012)

I am grateful to Pieter Kwant, a friend who is also my agent, for generating the idea of this book, and to Kathleen Scott Goldingay for commenting on the first draft.

INTRODUCTION

This book covers the twelve prophets whose names are attached to the last twelve books in the First Testament. We usually call them prophetic *books*, but they are nothing like what we mean by books. They would originally have been separate documents, and I often call them scrolls, though they were eventually compiled into one big scroll and incorporated into what Jews call "the Torah, the Prophets, and the Writings" and Christians came to call "the Old Testament."

The twelve are often called the "Minor Prophets," but there's nothing minor about them. Quite likely that title originally meant "shorter prophets," which gives you more the idea. When you put them all together, they are about the length of one of the "Major Prophets"—that is, the longer prophetic scrolls that bear the names of Isaiah, Jeremiah, and Ezekiel. Page for page, they are at least as challenging, thought-provoking, and encouraging as the big three.

I deal with the twelve scrolls in the order they come in the First Testament. The sequence is partly historical but partly not; we don't know for sure why they appear in the order they do. It doesn't make a lot of difference, though the way particular scrolls come together sometimes makes for interesting links. Within the treatment of individual scrolls, sometimes I cover the chapters in the order in which they come, but sometimes I vary the order. At the end of this book there's an index to enable you to find the discussion of particular chapters and sections.

The story of Israel as the First Testament tells it begins with Moses and the rescue of the Israelites from Egypt in about 1275 BC and extends to the rescue of Jerusalem from Antiochus Epiphanes in about 164 BC, as promised in the visions in Daniel. The prophets lived through the middle part of that period. Here's a tiny bit more historical background.

The country that is now occupied by Israel and Palestine is the area that was once promised to Abraham and was eventually occupied as "the land of Israel" by David and Solomon. In their day Israel was also the center of a little empire, but after Solomon it came to divide into two. The name of the southern part, including Jerusalem, was Judah. The northern part was much bigger, and it inherited the name Israel. So the names are confusing, because Israel is sometimes the name of the people of God and the land as a whole, sometimes just the name of the northern nation. The prophets also often call the northern nation Ephraim, so it's less confusing to think of the two peoples as Judah and Ephraim. Both nations were small compared with Egypt to the southwest, or with the big imperial powers in the region of modern Iraq and Iran, to the northeast: Assyria, then Babylon, then Persia (Assyria is also to be distinguished from Syria). Both nations occupied mostly mountain areas where life was tough. Growing enough food to eat was hard work; conceiving and bearing children was hard and dangerous work; relationships with the other peoples around were hard work; relationships with the imperial powers (and paying their taxes) were hard work.

Here's the possible historical order of the twelve prophets:

- Jonah, Amos, and Hosea worked in Ephraim in the eighth century—the years running up to the Assyrian conquest of the country.

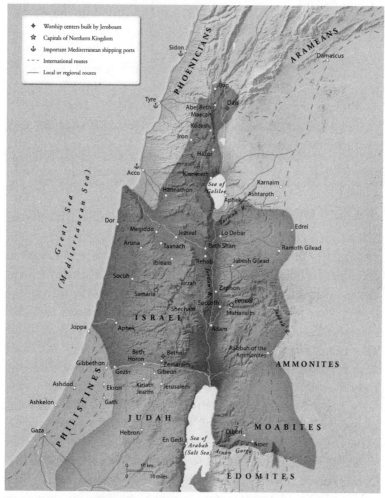

Ephraim and Judah in the time of Hosea, Joel, Amos, and Obadiah

- Micah worked in Judah in that same century—the years running up to an Assyrian invasion of Judah (and the same period as Isaiah).
- Nahum, Habakkuk, and Zephaniah worked in Judah in the seventh century—the years running up to the

Babylonian conquest of Judah (and the same period as Jeremiah).
- Obadiah worked in Judah in the mid-sixth century—the years after the Babylonian conquest (and the same period as Ezekiel, though he was in Babylon).
- Haggai and Zechariah worked in Judah in the late-sixth century—just after the Persians took over from the Babylonians.
- Joel and Malachi worked in Judah in the fifth century, and the story of Jonah was told in the same period.

In the First Testament, the prophetic scrolls are to some extent anthologies, in the sense that some of them include the messages of more than one prophet. Isaiah is the most obvious example. Isaiah 44:28–45:1 speaks of a Persian emperor, King Cyrus, as a figure of the present, not a figure of the future, but he lived two centuries after Isaiah. So there was more than one "Isaiah." Another odd thing is that there is a message in Isaiah 2:2–4 that also appears in Micah 4:1–3. Yet another odd thing is that Mark's Gospel begins with a quotation that he says comes from Isaiah, but the first half is actually from Malachi. So we shouldn't make too many assumptions about what it means when a prophetic scroll starts "the word of Yahweh that came to such-and-such a prophet." But the questions raised by these phenomena don't need to affect the exercise of imagination involved in this book, and I will treat each scroll in light of the person whose name appears at the beginning of it.

I should say something about that name Yahweh, too. This was the name that God gave to Moses and the Israelites for them to relate to him by. But it can seem a slightly odd, esoteric, hard to pronounce kind of name, and there's some danger of saying it lightly, and eventually the Jews gave up saying it and started using the ordinary word for "the Lord" instead. And when the First Testament got translated into other languages,

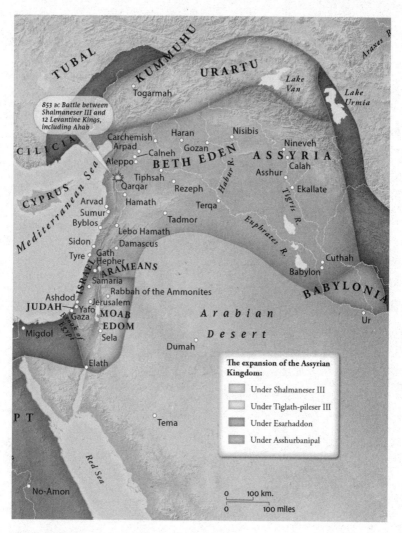

Judah and Assyria in the time of Jonah

the translators used their word for Lord whenever they came across the name. Most English translations work that way, printing the word as LORD so you can tell when the text is actually using the name Yahweh, though occasionally using the name Jehovah (another form of the same name). The drawback is that we can lose something of the point in a passage if we don't realize that the passage is using God's name (imagine if we never used the name Jesus!). So I keep the name Yahweh instead of replacing it.

LETTERS TO HOSEA

Hosea comes first among the twelve shorter prophets, perhaps because it is the longest. Like Jonah, Hosea came from Ephraim rather than Judah, and specifically he worked in the last decades of Ephraim's life before the Assyrians invaded the country and terminated its life as a nation. The dates are about the 750s to the 720s BC. In effect, Hosea tells you why that disaster happened. There were political reasons; the Assyrians wanted to get control of this area that was important from a trading point of view, and Ephraim wanted to keep its independence.

But Hosea is more interested in the religious factors that threaten the life of the nation. So he spends his time upbraiding Ephraim for its unfaithfulness to Yahweh, the God of Israel, who is the real God. He portrays the relationship between Yahweh and Israel as a marriage—an old-fashioned marriage in which the husband has the formal power in the relationship and is responsible for seeing that the family has enough to eat. But Ephraim looks to other "masters" for its needs: the term for these other gods, Baal, means "master," and it is also the formal word for a husband as the person who has that power in a family. Ephraim thus fails to treat Yahweh as its "husband." Yahweh bids Hosea turn his own life into an enacted parable, to try to get Ephraim to see what is going on.

1

[1:2]As the beginning of Yahweh's word through Hosea, Yahweh said to Hosea, 'Go get yourself a whorish woman and whorish children, because the country is really whoring away from Yahweh.' [3]So he went and got Gomer bat Diblayim.

She got pregnant and gave birth to a son for him. [4]Yahweh said to him, 'Name him "Jezreel," because in yet a little while I shall attend to the bloodshed in Jezreel upon Jehu's household. I shall stop the kingship of Israel's household. [5]On that day I shall break Israel's bow in Jezreel Vale.'

[6]She got pregnant again and gave birth to a daughter. He said to him, 'Name her "Not-Compassioned," because I shall no more have compassion again on Israel's household, that I should carry them.' . . .

[8]She weaned Not-Compassioned, got pregnant, and gave birth to a son. [9]He said, 'Name him "Not-My-People," because you're not my people and I—I shall not be God to you.' (1:2–9)

The nation's capital was Samaria, and Hosea mentions Samaria more often than Beth-El, where the most important sanctuary in Ephraim was. So I take it that he lived in Samaria. But he does refer to Beth-El, which had a proud history going back to Abraham and Sarah (Genesis 12:8; 28:10–22; 31:13). He also refers to Gilgal, the sanctuary down by the River Jordan that commemorated the Israelites' original crossing into Canaan (see Joshua 3–4). He makes a number of references to political events in his day without naming names, but allusions in 2 Kings 13–17 and in Assyrian records enable us to guess at some of the dates and names. Here are the kings during his time (the actual dates are approximate). The list gives you an impression of the kind of time it was.

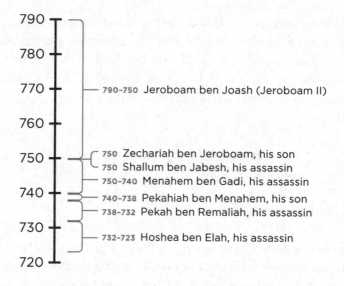

790
780
770 — 790–750 Jeroboam ben Joash (Jeroboam II)
760
750 ⎧ 750 Zechariah ben Jeroboam, his son
     ⎩ 750 Shallum ben Jabesh, his assassin
       — 750–740 Menahem ben Gadi, his assassin
740 — 740–738 Pekahiah ben Menahem, his son
     — 738–732 Pekah ben Remaliah, his assassin
730 — 732–723 Hoshea ben Elah, his assassin
720

Jeroboam's long reign was prosperous as well as stable, and in his reign Ephraim recovered land that had been taken over by Syria. The success fulfilled a promise from Yahweh through Jonah (2 Kings 14:23–29), which my imaginary letter from Jonah to Hosea refers to. But after Jeroboam's day it was all downhill as the Assyrians got interested in exercising more control of the region near the Mediterranean, with its trading possibilities. In Pekah's day that also meant pressure on Judah (2 Kings 16), as Isaiah 7 reports. His successor, Hoshea, was the last king of Ephraim: it was in his reign that the Assyrians brought the nation's life to an end, as Hosea threatened. (Ironically, Hoshea's name is actually the same as Hosea's, though the names come out differently in English translations.)

In these letters that follow, many of the other names and the links issue from my imagination and guesswork. They give you an idea of the relationship between Hosea's prophecies and the events of his day, rather than necessarily implying a proposal about the actual history. An exception are the letters from Maacah and Jaaziel. The background to their letters lies in Hosea's actual words in Hosea 5:8–14, which I include in the responses from Hosea that follow their letters.

A Letter to Hosea from Miriam bat Gedaliah, Wife of Diblaim ben Shobab

To my lord Hosea ben Beeri:

I thought I should write to tell you that my husband is depositing an affidavit with the elders of the City of Samaria concerning your abusive relationship with our daughter Gomer and her children.

Six years ago, your father and mother negotiated with us for you to become betrothed to Gomer. We knew that you belonged to the conservative group in Samaria, which is rigorous in its commitment to Yahweh. We also knew that there aren't many of you in that group and that you would have a hard time finding a bride from there. You knew that we are more open-minded people, though we are committed to Yahweh.

My husband is on King Jeroboam's staff and has to take part on the king's behalf in negotiations between Ephraim and other peoples, such as the Syrians. Relations between us and the Syrians are fraught and delicate. Ephraim once controlled Syria, then we were recurrently involved in conflict with the Syrians, then we got control of the area again. We now have a non-aggression pact with them, and you know that nations can't make treaties without both sides swearing that they will be faithful and saying "Amen" to each other's prayers, which each side addresses to its own deity. And we are aware that you and your conservative friends don't approve of that. In fact, you think Ephraim ought to be trusting in Yahweh and not making treaties with foreigners at all. But my husband takes the view that we have to live in the real world.

You were aware of all that, and you knew what kind of family Gomer came from, and yet you still got your parents to negotiate her betrothal to you. I realize that you believed that Yahweh told you to marry someone from this background and that, in a sense, you had no choice. And we thought that she might calm you down and get you to be a bit less narrow-minded, a bit more realistic about life. Not only have we been wrong, but you've gotten worse. So you called our beautiful granddaughter "Not-Compassioned." What a name for a child! I know you didn't mean it was this little girl who was not-compassioned, any more than her two brothers were. But what do you think that name will do for her when she goes to school? "Jezreel" was an odd name for the older one, as well. And the message you attached to it, about calamity coming to King Jeroboam as the current member of King Jehu's line, was seditious. It was also pretty implausible, given that King Jehu was anointed by the prophet Elisha. Don't you see you were contradicting another prophet of whom you approve? Then there was your most recent baby, whom you called "Not-My-People." That was the worst of the names, though at least it's obviously not a description of the child, in the way that "Not-Compassioned" sounds as if it is.

We have now heard that you threaten to divorce Gomer. There are no grounds in the Torah for your doing so. She has not been unfaithful to you. And you do not threaten to divorce her discreetly. You threaten to shame her publicly, when she has done nothing to deserve it except be our daughter. Your behavior is not in keeping with the alleged vocation of someone who claims to be a servant of Yahweh. And my husband is set on bringing you before the elders.

From the prophet Hosea ben Beeri
To Miriam bat Gedaliah:

> ^{2:2}She must put away her whoring from her face,
>   her adultery from between her breasts.
> ³Otherwise I shall strip her naked,
>   and turn her into like the day she was born.
> I shall make her like the wilderness,
>   change her into dry land, let her die of thirst.
> ⁴On her children I shall have no compassion,
>   because they're whorish children.
> ⁵Because their mother has been whorish;
>   the one who conceived them has acted
>   shamefully.
> Because she's said,
>   'I'll go after my lovers,
> The ones who give me my bread and my water,
>   my wool and my linen, my oil and my drink.'
>
> ⁶Therefore, here am I,
>   I'm going to hedge up your way with
>   thorn-bushes,
> And I shall build a wall for her,
>   so she can't find her paths.
> ⁷She'll pursue her lovers but she won't catch them,
>   she'll look to them but she won't find them.
> And she'll say,
>   'I'll go and return to my first man,
>   because it was better for me then than now.'
> ⁸She—she hasn't acknowledged
>   that I myself am the one who gave her
>   the grain, the new wine, and the fresh oil.
> I produced an abundance of silver for her,
>   and gold, which they used for the Master.

⁹Therefore, I shall take back
  my grain in its season and
  my new wine at its set time.
I shall rescue my wool and my linen
  for covering her nakedness.
¹⁰Now I shall uncover her villainy
  before her lovers' eyes.
No one will rescue her from my hand,
  ¹¹and I shall make all her celebrating stop,
Her festival, her new month, her sabbath,
  every set event of hers.
¹²I shall devastate her vine and her fig tree,
  of which she's said, 'It's my "gift,"
  which my lovers gave me.' . . .
¹³ᵇShe's decked herself with her ring and her
      jewellery,
  gone after her lovers,
  and put me out of mind (Yahweh's
      declaration). (2:2–13)

Background and Foreground

Hosea's audience would initially get the impression that Hosea is talking about a woman who is distinctively promiscuous, and it might make them tut-tut about her or about him. They have then fallen into his trap, because it soon becomes clear that he is talking about the people of Ephraim in general. When Yahweh tells him to marry a woman who is tainted by "whoring," by promiscuity, it need not imply her personal promiscuity, now or later. She need only be an ordinary Ephraimite girl who as such is more-or-less inevitably identified with the unfaithfulness to Yahweh that would characterize an ordinary Ephraimite family. The point is, then, that she stands for the people as a whole. They were using images in their worship of Yahweh and/or praying to other deities as well as Yahweh for his blessing on their crops and on the women's capacity to have children. The nation was also allying with other peoples for political ends and was involved in recognizing those other peoples' deities in solemnizing treaties with them. Yahweh is not going to let them continue that way. He will deprive them of the things that were actually his gifts and drive them to turn back to him.

A Letter to Hosea from Gomer bat Diblaim

To my lord Hosea ben Beeri:

My mother has shown me your response to her letter about me and you and Jezreel and Not-Compassioned and Not-My-People. We're all back with my father and mother now, and they like having us all with them. You know how grandparents are. But it's odd for us and I hate it and Jezreel is old enough to miss you and to ask questions about it all, and you know how people will gossip about a woman who has been thrown out by her husband, and how cruel children can be to other children who seem to be in an odd family situation. And in the long run, when my mother and father are old or when they have passed and the family is under the leadership of my brothers, it will put us all in a vulnerable position.

My parents have found a man who is willing to have me as his second wife. His wife hasn't been able to have children, and he knows I can become pregnant (of course it may turn out that he is the one who has the problem!). His wife is obviously hurt that he has to get another wife, but she gets on okay with me and I get on okay with her. My parents think he is a good man and will treat us reasonably and will treat the children as his own. But I don't look forward to it. He has given them the marriage endowment, but everything is not quite sealed and put into effect yet.

And I love you and I still don't really understand why you threw us all out. I know you see me and my family and my people as polluted by being willing to turn to the gods at the shrines and by the fact that my parents had prayed to the gods when they were hoping they would have me. And they had then prayed to them for a safe birth for me and my mother, and it seemed that their prayers were answered. But couldn't you have compassion on us now? You've made your point about faithfulness to Yahweh. Indeed, isn't there a point to be made about Yahweh's own faithfulness? Notwithstanding the name you gave to our daughter, Not-Compassioned, Yahweh is a God who is characterized by compassion, after all. My mother and I have been thinking about your requirement that we should be committed exclusively to Yahweh alone, in a strict sense. I'm not sure my father can handle the idea (it's impractical for him, anyway, as someone on the king's staff). But my mother and I can see that you may be right, and I might be willing to commit myself to you and to Yahweh in this way.

From the prophet Hosea ben Beeri
To Gomer bat Diblaim:

> 3:1Yahweh said to me further, 'Go, love a woman who is loved by a neighbour and who commits adultery— like Yahweh's love for the Israelites, though they're turning their face towards other gods and loving raisin slabs.' 2So I bought her for myself for fifteen silver pieces, a barrel of barley, and half a barrel of barley. 3I said to her, 'For a long time you're to live for me. You will not go whoring; you will not belong to a man. So also will I be for you.' 4Because for a long time the

Israelites are to live with no king, no official, no sacrifice, no pillar, no ephod or effigies. [5]Afterwards the Israelites will turn back and have recourse to Yahweh their God and David their king. They will be in dread of Yahweh and of his goodness at the end of the time. (3:1–5)

[4:13]On the tops of the mountains they sacrifice,
    on the hills they burn incense,
Under oak, poplar, and terebinth,
    because its shade is good.
That's why your daughters whore,
    your brides commit adultery.
[14]I shall not attend to your daughters because they
        whore,
        or to your brides because they commit
        adultery.
Because the men themselves consort with whores
    and sacrifice with hierodules,
    and a people that doesn't understand comes to
        ruin. (4:13–14)

[2:14]I'm going to charm her,
    and get her to go into the wilderness, and
        speak to her heart.
[15]I shall give her vineyards from there,
    Trouble Vale as Hope's Door.
She'll answer there as in her young days,
    as in the day she went up from the country of
        Egypt.
[16]On that day (Yahweh's declaration) she'll call,
        'My Man';
    she'll no more call me 'My Master.'

> ¹⁷I shall remove the Masters' names from her
> 　　mouth;
> 　they'll be mentioned by their name no
> 　　more. . . .
> ¹⁹I shall marry you to me permanently,
> 　marry you to me with faithfulness and with
> 　　the exercise of authority,
> With commitment and with compassion,
> 　²⁰marry you to me with truth. . . .
> ²³I shall have compassion on Not-Compassioned,
> 　and I shall say to Not-My-People 'My people'
> 　and it will say 'My God.' (2:14–20, 23)

Background and Foreground

Hosea's scathing words about Ephraim's fathers and husbands and about their daughters and brides make more explicit that the object of his attack is not the women of Ephraim, certainly not them alone. Paradoxically, Gomer stands for the men. They have to see themselves in her. If they are the people who determine religious and political policy in Ephraim, they are the people who have some responsibility for encouraging practices such as the womenfolk praying to deities other than Yahweh when they want to get pregnant and praying to them for safe delivery. The men would see themselves as upright members of the community. Actually, says Hosea, they themselves are involved in adultery. The men are whores. But Yahweh's threat to throw them out from his presence is not the end of the story. His willingness to have them back is enacted by Hosea when he has Gomer back instead of surrendering her to another man who would like to marry her. Now she is to be irrevocably faithful to him, and he will be irrevocably faithful to her. And that will mirror-image the relationship of Yahweh and Ephraim.

A Letter to Hosea from Libni ben
Amram, Priest in Samaria

To my lord Hosea ben Beeri:

My brother priests and I write to offer some remarks on your ministry here in Samaria. We much appreciate your critique of people like the Assyrians. In a context in which we are under pressure from imperial powers like them, we are encouraged by your assuring the people of Ephraim that Yahweh will not tolerate the peoples of the world forever, in their lack of truthfulness in their relations with us, their lack of commitment to us, and their refusal to acknowledge God. From reports that our merchants and diplomats bring back, we know that the life of the Assyrians is riddled by fraud, deception, theft, adultery, and violence. It has been a reassurance to us to hear you affirm that Yahweh is going to act in judgment against them.

On the other hand, we must protest at the critique you go on to, when you critique us as priests. We are the appointed servants of Yahweh and of his people in Ephraim. Our fathers and grandfathers and ancestors have been serving Yahweh and his people here for over two centuries. Some people think that you yourself are just a johnny-come-lately, self-appointed preacher. We believe you have no right to comment on our ministry in the way you have, and you should stop. And I address not just you, but the little group of upstarts who support you. You say that the spirit comes upon you. Some people say you are just crazy. You describe us as foolish and irresponsible and disbelieving in the teaching we give the people and in the advice we give the administration. We say that you are the dimwit for the reckless, negligent, quietist stance you commend, suggesting that we can conscientiously do nothing and let the Assyrians trample over Ephraim without taking any responsibility before God for our fate. You say that you have had visions from Yahweh, but you are not the only one to make claims like that, and saying you have had visions proves nothing. Some of Ephraim's alleged visionaries are the people who inspire the internal political strife, the coups and the assassinations that we have experienced as a nation and that you rightly deplore.

The nation needs the stability and respect for law that the priestly order undergirds. You cannot expect to get away with attacking us. And for the sake of the nation, we will see that you and your friends have to stop. If you are not afraid for yourselves, take note that we will see that your family suffers, too.

From the prophet Hosea ben Beeri
To Libni ben Amram, priest in Samaria:

> 4:6My people are terminated
>   for lack of acknowledgement.
> Because you've rejected acknowledgement
>   I shall reject you from being a priest for me.
> You've put out of mind your God's instruction;
>   I shall put out of mind your children, I too.
> 7As they became many, so they did wrong to me;
>   I shall exchange their honour for slighting.
> 8They feed on my people's wrongdoing;
>   they direct its appetite to their waywardness.
> 9So it will be: as the people, so the priest;
>   I shall attend to its ways for it. (4:6–9)

> 5:4Their practices don't allow them
>   to turn back to their God.
> Because there's a whorish spirit within them,
>   and they don't acknowledge Yahweh.

⁵ Israel's majesty will avow against it;
   so Israel and Ephraim will collapse through
     their waywardness. . . .
⁶They may go out with their flock and with their
     cattle,
   to seek Yahweh.
But they won't find him—he's withdrawn
     from them;
   ⁷they've broken faith with Yahweh.
Because they've given birth to alien children,
   the new moon will now consume their shares.
     (5:4–7)

^{9:7b} Israel must acknowledge it, though the prophet is
     stupid,
   the person of the spirit is crazy,
On account of the abundance of your
     waywardness,
   your abundant animosity.
⁸A prophet, with my God,
   is a lookout over Ephraim.
There's a hunter's snare over all his ways,
   animosity in its God's house.
⁹They've gone deep in devastation, as in the days
     at Gibeah;
   he'll be mindful of their waywardness, he'll
     attend to their wrongdoings. (9:7–9)

Background and Foreground

The opening part of the priest's letter reflects remarks Hosea had made about the world in general (4:1–3), but those comments were a lead-in or attention-getter before Hosea comes to indict the priests and Ephraim as a whole for failing to "acknowledge" Yahweh. This key verb often simply means "know," but "knowing the truth" is not a matter of theological understanding and "knowing God" is not a matter of having an intimate relationship or a rapport of heart. This "knowing" involves an acknowledging that entails a commitment of the life. The priests' vocation as pastors and teachers is to lead people in an acknowledgment of Yahweh, by their life and their teaching, but they don't fulfil that vocation. So in effect they prevent their people from turning back to Yahweh. They encourage people in their whoring instead of summoning them back, and they encourage them to pray to alien gods for the gift of children. They then see a prophet like Hosea, upon whom God's spirit comes, as someone crazy. *Sure I'm crazy,* Hosea says. *The combination of Yahweh's message and your attitude drives me crazy. My job as a prophet is to be a lookout, warning my people of danger that is coming, but they won't take any notice. Instead they try to trap me; they show animosity towards me.* Hosea is elsewhere negative about the kings of Ephraim, and "the days at Gibeah" might be the days when Israel first appointed a king (9:9; see 1 Samuel 8–15).

A Letter to Hosea from Maacah bat Ammiel in Gibeah

To my lord Hosea ben Beeri in Samaria:

You don't know us, but my sisters and I and our children have been in the temple courtyard during the festival at Beth-El and we have heard you describing your visions of an invasion, which might come from Assyria—or might come from Judah. It was frightening. Here we are, living and celebrating here in Beth-El near the border with Judah, and you pictured the Judahites invading us, even during the festival. They have their festival a month before us, of course, so we could imagine them having their celebration and then being all buoyed up to set off to give us what for. It would be cunning to attack when we ourselves were at our festival and the men were all the worse for drink.

You spoke as if the alarm needed to be sounded now, in the other places near the border that would be most vulnerable to invasion from Judah, places like our homestead near Gibeah. Invasion would mean finding that we went to bed as Ephraimites and woke up as Judahites. Or it would mean going to bed as people with our allocation of land and waking up as people who would be thrown off their land when it was taken over by some ambitious Judahite invaders. Or it would mean going to bed as people who were free and waking up as people who had lost our freedom as well as our means of livelihood.

It was funny and wily but alarming that you compared the despicable Judahite leaders to men creeping out at night to move the boundary markers between their family's land and another family's land so that they increased their holding, and we were encouraged when you promised that they will pay for it, too. But this doesn't help us much with the prospect of them actually doing it to us. It was also funny and wily but frightening the way you described Yahweh as like a moth. We women know how moths eat the family clothes, even eat the fabric we are weaving from our wool or our flax before we have chance to make something out of it. It was less funny and simply scary when you said that Yahweh was like a lion or a cougar, and you implied that what we need to fear isn't really an attack by the Judahites. It's an attack by this lion.

Of course, what we in Ephraim are inclined to do is firm up our alliances with the Syrians or the Assyrians to protect ourselves. But when my sisters and I talked about it while the

men were sleeping off the banquet and the drink, we started
recognizing that you might be right that alliances could protect
us from Judah but not from Yahweh. So our question is, what
do we need to do?

From the prophet Hosea ben Beeri
To Maacah bat Ammiel in Gibeah:

> 5:8Sound a horn in Gibeah,
>   a trumpet in Ramah.
> Raise a shout in Beth Aven,
>   after you, Benjamin.
> 9Ephraim will become a desolation
>   on the day of reproof.
> Against Israel's clans
>   I've made known something truthful.
> 10(Judah's officials have become like people who
>   move a boundary;
>   on them I shall pour out my outburst like
>   water.)
> 11Ephraim is oppressed, crushed by the exercise of
>   authority;
>   because he resolved to go after filth:
> 12I myself am like a moth to Ephraim,
>   like rot to Judah's household. . . .
> 15I shall go, I shall return to my place,
>   until they make restitution,
> And seek my face;
>   in their pressure they'll seek me urgently:
> 6:1'Come on, let's return to Yahweh,
>   because he's the one who tore, but he can
>   heal us.
> He strikes down, but he can bandage us;

²he can bring us to life after two days.
On the third day he can raise us up,
  so we can live before him.
³When we acknowledge, pursue the
    acknowledging of Yahweh,
  like dawn his coming out is sure.
He'll come to us like rain,
  like spring rain that waters earth.'
        (5:8–12; 5:15–6:3)

¹⁰:¹²Sow for yourselves for faithfulness,
    reap in proportion to commitment,
  till the tillable ground for yourselves.
It's time for inquiring of Yahweh, until he comes,
    and showers faithfulness for you. (10:12)

¹³:¹⁴From Sheol's hand I could redeem them,
    from death I could restore them.
Where would be your scourges, death,
    where your destruction, Sheol? (13:14)

Background and Foreground

The exhortation about sounding the horn is the warning that Maacah has referred to. It leads into Hosea's answer to Maacah's question about what the people need to do, where he emphasizes that verb "acknowledge." The exhortation about sowing for faithfulness replaces the talk of acknowledging with a metaphor; then the reference to inquiring of Yahweh gives people the literal reality again. And the saying about Yahweh being able to rescue from Sheol rephrases the earlier talk about bringing back to life. Sheol is the name of the place where you go when you die—it's not a place of suffering or punishment, just a place of (enforced!) rest. Yahweh points out that he could save them from ending up in Sheol before their time.

A Letter to Hosea from Jaaziel ben Zechariah, Secretary of State in Samaria

To my lord Hosea ben Beeri:

I have heard you preaching in the city square and proclaiming a message that is critical of King Menahem and his policies. Although I am on the king's staff, it doesn't mean I can't look at the political questions from more than one angle, and I want to express openly but confidentially to you the way I see things in Ephraim. The king himself believes in free speech and has no plan to take steps to stop you from preaching. But I am afraid that he will not take that stance forever, and I would like to explain the way I understand the government's policies in the hope that you may see that they are more reasonable than you imply and that in a context when compromise is necessary, they are in the interests of the nation.

For most of our lifetime, we have been free of domination from Assyria and thus free from having to pay imperial taxes. It's been a time of prosperity. We were fortunate that the great King Jeroboam ben Joash reigned in Ephraim for all those years of security and prosperity. But then Zechariah ben Jeroboam reigned for only six months before he was assassinated by Shallum ben Jabesh. In a way, you can't blame Shallum for undertaking the action he did—one can see the arguments that led him to it. King Jeroboam had been lucky, in that the Assyrians had been asleep through most of his reign. But Tiglath-pileser had got into power in Assyria, and the signs were that the Assyrians were going to be taking more interest in peoples like us on the trade route to the Mediterranean and Egypt.

The problem was that Zechariah thought the same way as his father: sit quiet and hope for the best. Shallum believed that we need to stand up to the Assyrians, and the policy he wanted

to implement was, "Let's ally with the Syrians against Assyria."
On the whole, the rest of the military didn't agree with him.
They saw this policy as fatally dangerous for Ephraim, and his
majesty King Menahem agreed with them. He believed that
Shallum therefore had to be put out of the way, and he under-
took secret negotiations with the Assyrians to see what would
be the price of their support. So Shallum lasted only a month
before his majesty King Menahem assassinated him.

Politically speaking, Shallum and his majesty King Menahem
were both half-right. Tiglath was indeed starting to take an interest in us, but his majesty King Menahem was able to buy them
off. The downside is that it has meant us having to pay imperial
taxes, so that all the families who seemed to be doing quite well
have had to pay something extra on top of the regular tithes and
the regular taxes to cover the costs of the Samaria administration. It has brought an end to the decades when people could
make ends meet reasonably easily and introduced a period when
things are tougher economically even for people who were doing
okay. And there's no sign of that coming to an end. But at least
his majesty's coup has introduced a period of stability in the
nation, after Zechariah and Shallum. It seems to me to enable us
to live in the least bad of possible worlds at the moment.

From the prophet Hosea ben Beeri
To Jaaziel ben Zechariah, Secretary of State:

> 5:13Ephraim saw its sickness,
>   Judah its sore.
> Ephraim went to Assyria,
>   it sent to the king who would argue.
> But that man won't be able to heal you;
>   he won't cure you of a sore.
> 14Because I shall be like a lion to Ephraim,
>   like a cougar to Judah's household.

I, I myself, will tear,
    and as I go I shall carry, and there'll be no one
        to rescue. (5:13–14)

8:8Israel has been swallowed up
    and they have now become among the
        nations,
Like an object that no one wants,
    9because they've gone up to Assyria.
A wild donkey on its own,
    Ephraim has hired lovers.
10Even when they hire among the nations,
    now I shall collect them.
They've writhed for a while
    because of the burden (king, officers). (8:8–10)

5:1bGive ear, royal household,
    because authority belongs to you.
Because you've been a snare to The Watchtower
      [Mizpah],
    you've spread a net over Tabor. (5:1b)

8:14Israel has put out of mind its maker
    and built palaces,
    (and Judah has built many fortified towns).
I shall send off fire to its towns,
    and it will consume its citadels. (8:14)

Background and Foreground

At different points within Hosea's time, Assyria, as the power to the northeast, and Egypt, as the power to the southwest, were either a threat to Ephraim or a possible source of support. For Hosea, they are therefore sometimes agents of Yahweh's disciplining Ephraim, sometimes false sources for the help for which Ephraim should actually look to Yahweh. Hosea has no sympathy for Jaaziel's dilemma. Looking to Assyria will not solve Ephraim's problems, not least because Yahweh is actually the source of those problems. Jaaziel, his colleagues, and their master King Menahem are a burden to their people. The king and his entourage are supposed to be the people who exercise proper governmental authority in Ephraim, but instead they themselves have been a snare and a hunter's net to their nation, partly through doing what seemed the politically smart thing. Mizpah in the south and Tabor in the north may be sanctuaries that were the locations of meetings with negotiating teams from other nations where treaties were made, and therefore places where Ephraimite politicians were engaged in illicit religious ceremonies as part of their diplomacy.

A Letter to Hosea from the Editor
of the *Samaria Times*

To my lord Hosea ben Beeri:

We are sending you advance copy of this op-ed piece we have received. You know that our policy is to publish a variety of views on matters of concern within the nation, but this one is explosive. We would be glad to have your comments for publication.

> *Is There Too Much Political Instability in Ephraim?* One of the great things about Ephraim is that we are not locked into the position of having a hereditary monarchy like the Judahites. Although the Judahites can choose which member of the royal family they will have as the next king, they have no option about which family he (or even she!) comes from. It has to be David's

line, and the members of that family are often incompetent. Here in Ephraim, when we think that the royal family is irredeemably inept, we can move to another royal family.

But the frequency and the associated violence with which we have been doing so in recent decades is excessive. After the great King Jeroboam ben Joash, it was only six months before his son Zechariah ben Jeroboam was assassinated by Shallum ben Jabesh. He lasted only a month before there was another military coup and Menahem ben Gadi assassinated him. Menahem's coup introduced a decade's peace and quiet in the nation, but his son Pekahiah wasn't so fortunate. He reigned in Samaria for just two years after his father's death. Maybe the time had come when there needed to be a change of policy. Anyway, Pekahiah was assassinated by Pekah ben Remaliah.

As usual, the coup was brought about from within the army, but sources suggest that civilian politicians were also involved—as usual. It meant Pekah reneged on his oath of allegiance to King Pekahiah, and thereby reneged on an oath he had taken before Yahweh. He formed a conspiracy with fifty people from across the Jordan, from Gilead. Sources say they slipped down the mountains to the Jordan, crossed over at the ford at Adam, twenty miles north of Jericho, and from there made their way quietly up into the mountains to Samaria and killed Pekahiah. Reports say that in addition they had the cooperation of some priests, who were also thereby reneging on the oath that they had taken before Yahweh to be loyal to the king. It is assumed that the Gileadites were opposed to the pro-Assyrian policy that Pekahiah had inherited from his father and that they also felt vulnerable to their neighbor Syrians. That change of regime has therefore issued in new developments in Ephraimite foreign policy, closer relations

with the Syrians, and collaboration in resisting the expansion
of Assyrian influence. That has consequences for Judah,
too, given that Ephraim and Syria want to involve them in
resistance to Assyria.

The question is, when is enough enough?

From the prophet Hosea ben Beeri
To the editor of the *Samaria Times*:

> 6:4What shall I do with you, Ephraim,
> what shall I do with you, Judah,
> When your commitment is like morning cloud,
> like dew going early?
>
> 5That's why I hewed them down with my prophets,
> killed them with the words of my mouth;
> with rulings against you, light goes out.
> 6Because I wanted commitment not sacrifice,
> acknowledgment of God more than burnt
> offerings.
> 7But they—as at Adam they transgressed the pact;
> there they broke faith with me.
> 8Gilead is a township of people who bring trouble,
> trailed in blood.
> 9The company of priests
> is like gangs waiting for someone.
> On the road to Shechem they commit murder,
> when they have committed deliberate
> wickedness.
> 10In Israel's household I have seen something
> horrible:
> Ephraim's whoring is there.

Israel has become defiled [11a](Judah, too);
    he has appointed a harvest for you. (6:4–11a)

[8:11]Because Ephraim has built many altars for
        wrongdoing;
    for it, they've become altars for wrongdoing.
[12]Though I write for it many things in my
        instruction,
    they've been thought of as alien.
[13]Though they offer sacrifices to me as gifts,
    and eat flesh,
Yahweh doesn't accept them;
    now he'll be mindful of their waywardness.
He'll attend to their wrongdoings;
    those people—they'll go back to Egypt.
      (8:11–13)

Background and Foreground

Hosea gives his own account of the coup, which is an expression of people's preferring to worship and engage in political action rather than acknowledge Yahweh and act faithfully. To put it another way, their political commitments involve worship because they take their oaths before God, but then they take political action that belies their pact and thus breaks faith with the oath they took in worship. So their commitment to Yahweh doesn't issue in anything. It's no more productive than the morning clouds that don't issue in any rain. And their breaking their word is an aspect of whoring in the sense of unfaithfulness. That's why Yahweh is getting a prophet like Hosea to declare that calamity is coming and to initiate its actual happening by announcing it. The light is going to go out for them. Yahweh asks himself what else is he to do? Giving them more teaching, more instruction, doesn't get him anywhere. So Yahweh tries a lament to see if he can get them to see sense.

A Letter to Hosea from the Editor
of the *Jerusalem Times*

To my lord Hosea ben Beeri in Samaria:

We are sending you advance copy of this news report. We would be glad to have your comments for publication.

Another Army Coup in Samaria. Authorities in Jerusalem are having trouble concealing a smile at news that King Pekah ben Remaliah has been assassinated in Samaria. It's not long since Pekah, along with Rezin the Syrian king, showed up in Jerusalem with a considerable force to lean on King Ahaz to join them in declaring independence of Assyria, with the threat that otherwise they might depose the king. Now it transpires that Pekah was not so secure on his own throne. Actually, past history in Ephraim should surely have made this clear to him. The wisdom of King Ahaz's refusal to join with Ephraim and Syria in standing up to Assyria was vindicated by the Assyrian invasion of Ephraim, which involved annexing the bulk of the northern and eastern part of the country and reducing Ephraim to a shadow of its former self. It's hardly surprising that it made Pekah vulnerable to a coup.

So in the usual Ephraimite fashion, people who had sworn loyalty to Pekah have reneged on their oath. The only surprise about this coup is that Pekah didn't see it coming and stay more alert, given that he was himself an experienced assassin, but it looks as if people like that somehow develop a sense of their own invincibility.

It seems that the conspirators had been shaping a plot for a while, but they brought it to fruition at a birthday party.

This has also caused smiles in Jerusalem, but it's possible that here King Ahaz is now being more careful about any celebratory meals that people suggest. In Samaria, the wine flowed and the king and his court were not holding back from it. The slayers were presumably being more restrained, but the king and his court didn't suspect anything. There was much conviviality and backslapping. And then there was the slaying.

With more irony, the assassin and new king is one Hoshea ben Elah, whose name is the same as that of the prophet who has been causing a stir in Samaria. Hoshea's policy will involve returning to an acceptance of Assyrian overlordship. Here in Jerusalem, rumor says that elements at court favor turning to Egypt for support over against Assyria. Experts here are wondering how long Hoshea's loyalty to Assyria will last and whether he will be turning to Egypt, too. Politically, it's easy to see where that will lead. The Assyrians will not tolerate it. They will invade, and they will cut Ephraim down even more. Those Gileadites will turn out to be right: they will find themselves taken off to Assyria to work for the Assyrians there. Hosea will turn out to be right to be asking questions about whether the future of Ephraim will be as positive as it was in his young days. Hoshea will be deposed and the country will be devastated.

Would you like to comment?

From the prophet Hosea ben Beeri in Samaria
To the editor of the *Jerusalem Times:*

> 7:3They make a king rejoice, with their bad dealing,
>   and officials, with their lies.
> 4All of them are committing adultery,

like an oven burning without a baker.
He stops stirring
    from the kneading of the dough to its yeasting.
⁵On our king's day,
    officials got sick with the heat of wine.
He extended his hand to the arrogant ⁶when they
        came near,
    their mind like an oven with intrigue.
All night their baker slept,
    in the morning he's burning, like a
        flaming fire.
⁷All of them burn as hot as an oven,
    they consume their authorities.
All their kings have fallen;
    there's no one among them calling to me.
        (7:3–7)

⁸:¹Horn to your mouth,
    like an eagle over Yahweh's house!
Since they've transgressed my pact,
    rebelled against my instruction.
²To me they cry out,
    'My God, as Israel we've acknowledged you.'
³Israel has rejected what's good;
    an enemy pursues them.
⁴ᵃThey've made kings, but not through me;
    they've made officials, but I haven't
        acknowledged them. (8:1–4a)

¹⁰:³Because they now say,
    'We have no king;
Because we do not live in awe of Yahweh,
    the King: what would he do for us?'
⁴They've spoken things with empty oaths,

in solemnizing a pact.
The exercise of authority has flourished like
poisonous growth
in the furrows of the field. (10:3–4)

$^{10:7}$Samaria—its king is being terminated,
like a twig on the face of water.
^{8}The shrines of Aven will be annihilated,
Israel's wrongdoing.
Thorn and thistle
will grow on their altars.
They will say to the mountains, 'Cover us,'
to the hills, 'Fall on us.' (10:7–8)

$^{13:9}$Your devastation, Israel,
because in me is your help.
^{10}Where is your king, then,
so he may deliver you in all your towns,
And your authorities, of whom you said,
'Give me a king and officials'?
^{11}I'd give you a king in my anger
and take him in my outburst. (13:9–11)

Background and Foreground

Hosea's message again gives his account of the coup. First,
the conspirators pledged their loyalty to the king and gave
him a false sense of security. Gastronomy was apparently then
involved in this assassination, and Hosea roguishly makes it
also a metaphor for the coup itself. While the chefs in Samaria
were preparing for the party, the conspirators were cooking up
a plot. The message about the coup concludes with a comment
on the long sequence of kings that have come and gone, without it ever leading to their turning to Yahweh. The subsequent
excerpts from Hosea's other messages express different angles

on the series of changes in kingship in Ephraim. There's the fact that they have kept appointing new kings, but not with Yahweh being involved in the process. There's the fact that they dismiss the idea of Yahweh being King; they wouldn't have openly said that, but it's implicit in the way they formulate their policies and the way they behave. There's the fact that the final disaster is definitely coming on Ephraim and that their king will be carried away like a twig in a stream (Aven, meaning "trouble" or "wickedness" is a pejorative name for Beth-El). To look at the appointment of kings another way, there's the fact that Yahweh was involved in the appointment and in the kings' removal, but it was a punitive involvement.

A Letter to Hosea from Adonijah ben Raham, Priest in Gilgal

To my lord Hosea ben Beeri in Samaria:

During the recent Sukkot festival in Gilgal, people have been muttering about what you are alleged to have said about our celebrations, here and in other sanctuaries. People come to Gilgal to give thanks for the harvest and to worship Yahweh. We gather to celebrate the gifts of barley and wheat from which we bake our bread, and the gift of water to irrigate the land, which comes out of the ground in the springs in our area. We gather to celebrate the gifts of wool from the sheep on the hills, which is so important for people who live up in the mountains where it's colder than down here, and of flax that we can weave to make fabric for the clothes that we all need. We gather to celebrate the harvest of the olive trees that provide us with oil for our bread and for our lamps, and grapes for our wine, and figs and dates so we have something sweet.

I know that people at the festival vary over whether their

focus is entirely on Yahweh. They know that Yahweh is the great God, and they may acknowledge that he is such a great God that he alone really deserves the description "God." But they also know that there are other supernatural beings apart from Yahweh, beings who are subordinate to Yahweh, and they may ask these other beings to help with the harvest as well as with the possibility of having a baby. So they are giving thanks to them at Sukkot, too. But it doesn't mean they don't believe in Yahweh.

We have been a sanctuary here by the Jordan since the earliest days of Israel. When we gather to celebrate the harvest, we also celebrate the way Yahweh has been our God through the centuries. We remember the way Yahweh took hold of our ancestors as his people. We remember the joy we brought to him. We remember how he got our ancestors out of Egypt and brought them through the wilderness. We process down to the Jordan to look at the rocks that commemorate our ancestors' crossing the river when they came into Canaan. We look across the river towards the area where they camped near Peor. It was the place where Balak the king of Moab tried to get an expert in divination called Balaam to curse the Israelites, but he blessed them instead. It was the area from where Moses was able to climb Mountain Nebo and survey the country.

It seems to me and my colleagues that your negative attitude to Gilgal means you are despising the story of Yahweh's great acts of faithfulness and power that brought us into this country. You should be encouraging people to come and celebrate and give thanks for what Yahweh did, not discouraging them.

From the prophet Hosea ben Beeri
To Adonijah ben Raham, priest in Gilgal:

> 4:15bDon't come to Gilgal, don't go up to Beth Aven
> ['Trouble House'],
>   don't swear 'As Yahweh lives!'

¹⁶Because like a defiant cow
    Israel has been stubborn. . . .
¹⁷ Ephraim is attached to images;
    leave him to himself. (4:15b–17)

^{9:1}Don't rejoice, Israel, with joy like the peoples,
    because you've gone whoring away from
        your God.
You have loved the 'gift'
    on every grain threshing-floor. . . .
³They won't live in Yahweh's country;
    Ephraim will go back to Egypt,
    in Assyria they'll eat defiled food.
⁴They won't pour wine for Yahweh;
    their sacrifices won't please him. . . .
⁵What will you do for the set day,
    for the Day of Yahweh's festival?
⁶Because there—when they have gone from
        destruction,
    Egypt will collect them, Memphis will
        bury them.
Whereas high regard will attach to their silver,
    briar will dispossess them, bramble will be in
        their tents. (9:1, 3–6)

^{9:10}I found Israel
    as like grapes in the wilderness.
I saw your fathers
    as like the first fruit on a fig tree in its
        beginning.
When those people came to the Master of Peor,
    they dedicated themselves to Shame,
    and became abominations like the thing they
        loved. . . .

¹⁵All their bad dealing was at Gilgal,
    because there I was hostile to them. (9:10, 15)

^{12:9}I am Yahweh your God
    from the country of Egypt.
I shall make you live in your tents again,
    as in the days of your set occasion. . . .
¹¹Is Gilead trouble: yes, emptiness;
    in Gilgal did they sacrifice bulls?
Their altars, too,
    are like stone heaps [*gallim*] on the furrows of
        the field. (12:9, 11)

Background and Foreground

Gilgal was a sanctuary down by the River Jordan, near Jericho. It was important as a crossing place at the foot of the road that came down from Beth-El (Beth Aven), in particular because it was the place where the Israelites crossed the Jordan with Joshua when they first came into Canaan. Hosea has two sorts of comment to make about Gilgal. One applies to all Ephraim's sanctuaries: he does not accept that it's okay to pray to beings other than Yahweh, even if people think of them as Yahweh's underlings. It's still like whoring. So Yahweh will terminate the sacrificing and the celebrating, and instead of the feast they'll be eating defiled food in exile in Assyria or in Egypt. As they lived in bivouacs on the way from Egypt and then lived in them during the festival to commemorate it, so they will again—but not as a form of celebration. As Gilgal's country goes wild, the Egyptians will be only too happy to bury its people and appropriate their valuables.

Hosea's other sort of comment about Gilgal is that it stands in a particular way for Ephraim's apostasy as well as for Yahweh's grace. Whereas the priest emphasizes the grace, Hosea emphasizes the apostasy. The priest refers to the Balaam story, which comes in Numbers 22–24, but ignores the Peor story to which Hosea refers, which follows in Numbers 25. At Peor the Israelites got involved in praying to Moabite gods. The closing allusion to Gilead and Gilgal may refer to the occasion noted in the *Samaria Times* letter and in Hosea 6. But here, Hosea also makes another roguish use of words: the altars in Gilead and Gilgal are just *gallim*, stone heaps, or soon will be.

A Letter to Hosea from Eleazar ben Azariah, Craftsman in Shechem

To my lord Hosea ben Beeri in Samaria:

I and my fellow craftsmen are offended by your attacks on our trade. All our lives we have been engaged in making things that contribute to people's worship. We learned our craft from our fathers, and we are proud to teach it to our sons. And our grandfathers, or rather, their ancestors several generations ago, made the great images at Beth-El and at Dan.

The images that we make are carved out of the finest wood, from trees that we carefully cultivate—we don't just use leftovers or offcuts or firewood or woodchips. We then paint them in bright colors that reflect the god's splendor, or we pass them on to our fellow-craftsmen in silver or gold who plate them in a way that makes them even more glorious.

You talk as if we were making idols, things that would be substitute deities for people. It's not true. We are making things of positive help to people in their spirituality. They are things that are not too otherworldly, objects that represent Yahweh and that people can relate to. You have to accept that people are made of flesh and blood, and the idea that God is just an ethereal being is hard for ordinary people to relate to. They need something they can see. You speak as if we think that the images we make actually are gods. Do you think we are stupid?

From the prophet Hosea ben Beeri
To Eleazar ben Azariah:

> 4:12My people asks things of its piece of wood;
>   its stick tells it.
> Because a whorish spirit has led it astray;
>   they've whored from under their God. (4:12)

> 8:4bWith their silver and gold they've made images for
>   themselves,
>   in order that [Israel] may be cut off.
> 5He's rejected your bullock, Samaria;
>   my anger burns against them.
> How long will they be incapable of being free of
>   guilt?—
>   6because it was from Israel.
> That thing—a metal worker made it;
>   it's not a god,
> Because Samaria's bullock
>   will become broken bits. (8:4b–6)

> 10:5The population of Samaria fear
>   for the bullock of Beth Aven,
> Because its people and its priestlings are
>   mourning over it
>   whereas they celebrate over its splendour.
> Because it's going into exile from it;
>   6it, too, will be brought to Assyria,
>   a gift to the king so he will argue.
> Ephraim will receive shame,
>   Israel will be shamed by its counsel. (10:5–6)

[13:1]When Ephraim spoke, there was trembling,
    when he lifted [his voice] in Israel,
      but through the Master he became liable
        and died.
[2]Now they commit more and more wrongdoing,
    and they've made themselves an idol,
Images from their silver in accordance with their
        insight,
    the work of craftsmen, all of it. . . .
[3]Therefore they will be like the morning cloud,
    like the dew that goes early,
Like chaff that whirls from a threshing floor,
    like smoke from a window. (13:1–3)

Background and Foreground

Ephraimites had several sorts of images, and Hosea and his fellow Ephraimites talk about images in several different ways. There are the bull images at the two chief sanctuaries at Dan and at Beth-El (Beth Aven, "Trouble House" or "Wickedness House"), which are destined to be smashed or to end up in Assyria. There are images at the local shrines (the "high places"). And there are images that people had at home. Some will be images of Yahweh; some will be images of other deities. Some people will make the distinction between the image and the thing it represents, as the craftsman does; for other people that distinction is too subtle. But anyway, Hosea himself doesn't make these distinctions. He declares that Yahweh views all of the images as despicable. The fundamental theological reason is that it's simply impossible to make a satisfactory image of Yahweh, the only real God. Yahweh is essentially a God who acts and speaks. An image can't represent that central nature of Yahweh. It's bound to be misleading. Even if someone thinks their image represents Yahweh, it's actually an image of something else. It's just a piece of wood.

A Letter to Hosea from Jonah
ben Amittay in Gat-hepher

To my lord Hosea ben Beeri in Samaria:

The years are passing here in Lower Galilee and times are changing. I'm enjoying my senior years, watching my sons look after the farm and the flocks and watching my grandchildren grow up. I continue to have a small prophetic ministry—people from the area around come to see me when they have a worry or a need and they want to know what Yahweh might say to them.

From where we are in Gat-hepher we're near the highway that runs northeast, to Syria and eventually Assyria, and that runs in the other direction across to the Mediterranean and eventually to Egypt. If I take a little walk I can see the merchant caravans making their way along the highway and the diplomatic caravans going either way, too. It keeps me thinking about that message that Yahweh gave me when we were under pressure from the Syrians, and he said we were going to put them in their place, and we did. It was a mystery, really, because we didn't deserve to. We weren't devoted to Yahweh. The country was prosperous through those years, too, though we didn't deserve that either, any more than we do now when things are getting economically tough. My sons worry about whether the grain harvest and the olive harvest will be good enough for them to be able to pay the taxes to Samaria so that Samaria can send what the Assyrians demand from us.

It makes me continue thinking about how Yahweh relates to us. As I say, we didn't deserve that victory over the Syrians. We hadn't been faithful in our relationship with Yahweh. We enjoyed our prosperity, but it made people less inclined to turn to Yahweh, rather than more inclined. They might go to Dan or Beth-El for the festival—from here there's not much difference in the distance. Going down via Samaria to Beth-El is exciting, but Dan is so pretty. The people would go through the motions of acknowledging Yahweh there, but back home I know they were also praying to the Masters. And I hear reports that you are telling people in Samaria that Yahweh is getting to the end of his tether about it. So I'm wondering how you see the relationship between Yahweh's love for us and his graciousness toward us, on one hand, and the need for him to act tough on the other. Do you think he will always be committed to us?

From the prophet Hosea ben Beeri
To the prophet Jonah ben Amittay:

> 11:1When Israel was a boy I loved him;
> 　　from Egypt I called my son.
> 2I called them;
> 　　thus they went from me.
> They sacrifice to the Masters,
> 　　burn incense to images.
> 3I myself taught Ephraim to walk,
> 　　lifted them into my arms.
> But they didn't acknowledge
> 　　that I healed them.
> 4With human cords I would lead them,
> 　　with loving ties.
> For them I was
> 　　someone lifting a baby to the cheek,
> 　　and I bent to him so that I might feed him.
>
> 5No, they'll go back to the country of Egypt,
> 　　or Assyria will be their king,
> 　　because they refused to come back.
> 6A sword will whirl against its towns,

finish off its gate-bars, consume them because
of their counsels.
⁷My people are bent on turning back from me;
when they call to the One on High,
he won't lift them up at all.

⁸How can I give you up, Ephraim,
hand you over, Israel?
How can I make you like Admah,
treat you like Zeboim?
My spirit turns round within me,
my comfort warms all at once.
⁹I shall not act on my angry burning;
I shall not again devastate Ephraim.
Because I am God and not a human being,
the sacred one among you,
and I shall not come against the town.
¹⁰They will follow Yahweh;
he will roar like a lion.
When he roars,
children will come trembling from the west.
¹¹They will come trembling like a bird from
Egypt,
like a pigeon from the country of Assyria,
I shall let them live in their homes (Yahweh's
declaration). (11:1–11)

Background and Foreground

Jonah knew that Yahweh loved Israel and that he loved
them and cared for them even when they didn't deserve it.
He had given Jonah a promise about deliverance and success
for Ephraim, even when they were unfaithful (the story is
in 2 Kings 14:23–27). So what is the relationship between
Yahweh's grace and his expectations of people's faithfulness?

Hosea's message suggests a perspective on Jonah's question. It's possible to stop before the end of his message, after the line about being God and not a human being and therefore letting grace have the last word (11:9). But Hosea doesn't stop there. When Isaiah gives his account of his commission as a prophet (Isaiah 6), it's easy to stop halfway through with a warm feeling ("Here I am, send me"; 6:8) and thereby avoid the tough continuation of the passage. It's the same with the story of Samuel's commission (1 Samuel 3:9; "Speak, Yahweh, because your servant is listening."). It's again easy to stop halfway through the message. Here Hosea speaks of the way Yahweh holds back from acting against Ephraim because he's not like a human being who acts on his wrath. And it's easy to stop reading there. But Hosea goes on to speak more of Ephraim's lying and deceit, which means that the relenting does not have the last word in Hosea's message. From this message, Ephraim can be sure that Yahweh will relent if it turns to Yahweh. But if it does not. . . .

A Letter to Hosea from Amaziah, Senior Priest of Beth-El

To my lord Hosea ben Beeri in Samaria:

As you know, I have more contact with the prophet Amos from Judah than I have with you. He is in Beth-El more often than you are, but he wisely keeps out of Samaria as the nation's capital. I am hopeful that he may take my advice and stay on his side of the frontier between Judah and Ephraim. But I hear that you issue critiques and threats relating to Beth-El, even in Samaria, and it is for that reason that I write to ask you to desist.

Here at Beth-El, we are proud of our connection with Abraham and Jacob. Our sanctuary was one of the first places where Abraham and Sarah stopped when they first came to Canaan. They built an altar here and called on Yahweh here and thus put a special mark on this place, long before anyone thought about the little town of Jerusalem being important. And this was the place where God appeared to Abraham and Sarah's grandson Jacob when he was on his way back to Mesopotamia. This was the place where God confirmed his promise to him that he would be the fountainhead of a people who would experience the blessing promised to Abraham and be the means of blessing all the nations. Jacob set up a pillar here to commemorate God appearing to him, and when he returned to Canaan, God made a point of telling him to come back here.

This is a sacred place and a place that Yahweh has made significant in Israel's story. You have no right to be accusing it of being a place that does not stand for faithfulness to Yahweh. You are belittling Yahweh. You must please stop.

From the prophet Hosea ben Beeri
To Amaziah, priest of Beth-El:

> 12:2Yahweh will argue with Judah,
>> and attend to Jacob in accordance with
>>> his ways;
>> in accordance with his practices he will give
>>> back to him.
> 3In the womb he grabbed his brother,
>> and in his strength he struggled with God.
> 4He struggled with the envoy and prevailed;
>> he cried and sought grace from him.
> He would find him at Beth-El,
>> speak with him there,
> 5Yahweh, God of Armies—
>> Yahweh is his name.

[6]So you yourself are to turn back to your God;
keep watch on commitment in the exercise of
authority,
and wait for your God always.

[7]A trader in whose hand are deceptive scales
loves to defraud.
[8]Ephraim has said, 'Yes, I've become rich,
I've acquired strength for myself.
In all that I've toiled for they won't find in me
waywardness that amounts to wrongdoing.'
(12:2–8)

[12:12]Jacob fled to the open country of Aram [Syria];
Israel served for a wife—
for a wife he kept [sheep].
[13]Through a prophet Yahweh got Israel up from
Egypt,
and through a prophet he was kept.
[14]Ephraim provoked with great bitterness;
his Lord will leave his bloodshed on him,
give back his reviling to him. (12:12–14)

Background and Foreground

As Gilgal is proud of its significance in Israel's story and of being a key sanctuary, Bethel is proud of its significance in Israel's story and even more proud of its status (along with Dan) as one of the two national sanctuaries (see 1 Kings 12). But at the very least, Amaziah needs to think about the clash between Jacob the hero and Ephraim the nation that is so proud of itself and deceives itself about its waywardness (Hosea 12:8). There are some further implicitly snide implications in what Hosea says. The word "trader" is also the word for "Canaanite," and one could easily think of the Ephraimites as quasi-Canaanite in the way they pray to the Masters, the Baals. And the proverb about traders (12:7) hints at the idea that no one gets rich through being involved in trading without doing a spot of cheating people.

Yet further, Hosea can put a less positive spin on Beth-El's story than its priest does, as he can on Gilgal's. There are elements in Jacob's story that Amaziah omits. What about the way Jacob grabbed his brother by the heel in the womb in order to try to get ahead of Esau (Genesis 25:21–26)? What about the way he struggled with God when God appeared to him, as he was on his way back to meet Esau again, scared stiff (32:22–32)? At best, these stories are ambiguous about the kind of person Jacob was. Nor does Hosea make all the points that could be made about Jacob as someone "deceptive," like the trader's scales. It was Isaac's description of him when he pretended to be Esau in order to get Isaac to give him Esau's inheritance (Genesis 27:35). Ironically, "deception" is also a word Genesis applies to Jacob's sons when they engage in a murderous strategy against the men of Shechem (34:13). Where did they inherit that quality from?! And "deceive" or "beguile" is the verb he applies to his father-in-law when Laban foists Leah on him instead of Rachel, as he is engaged in keeping sheep in order to earn the "gift" of a wife (29:25). So either Jacob is a hero of whom Ephraim is unworthy, or the Ephraimites are worthy descendants of Jacob the deceiver.

The "prophet" whom Hosea mentions (Hosea 12:13) is Moses, and God's continuing to fulfill his commitment to Jacob by "keeping" Jacob's family or flock (that is, Israel) adds to the enormity of his descendants' waywardness—the political violence that stains it and the reviling of Yahweh that's implicit in the way it turns to other so-called deities instead of Yahweh. They will have their natural consequences.

A Letter to Hosea from Ulam ben Micah

To my lord Hosea ben Beeri:

My name will mean nothing to you; I am simply an Ephraimite who works for the administration in Samaria. I have listened to you preaching in the city square and I know you are right in much of your critique of Ephraim for its unfaithfulness to Yahweh.

You won't be surprised to know that we are not at the end of the political consequences of the tumults of the last two or three years. First, we had the change in our policy about relationships with Assyria. We had been paying taxes to them in return for their support of King Menahem, but after King Pekahiah succeeded him, many people thought it was time to resist that arrangement. That was what lay behind King Pekah's assassination of King Pekahiah. But in order to have more of a joint front in standing firm against the Assyrians, we made an alliance with the Syrians and tried to get the Judahites to join in. Of course, that's where the plan backfired. Instead, the wretched Judahites themselves appealed to Assyria for support against us.

That exposed our second miscalculation. While intelligence had told us that Tiglath-pileser was a much more energetic emperor than his predecessor and also that he had vast ambitions, precisely because he had those vast ambitions we didn't think he would be too interested in us. We were wrong. It was the greatest political miscalculation in our history. The horrific invasion that followed meant that the Assyrians simply annexed the northern and eastern half of the country and made it subject to direct Assyrian rule. They also took many people to Assyria as forced migrants—they took people involved in the administration, craftsmen, and so on. No government could survive such a disaster, and no imperial authorities could simply leave a rebel king on the throne. So we had yet another military coup, either instigated or countenanced by the Assyrians, King Pekah was executed, and King Hoshea took the throne with the Assyrians' approval.

And I got a job with King Hoshea's administration. I was appointed to the party that went to Calah to accompany our tax payments to the Assyrians. But now Tiglath has died and policy has changed again and once more we are joining with other peoples in the far west of the Assyrian Empire in stopping paying those imperial taxes and seeking alliance with Egypt (no doubt we will find we are paying taxes to the Egyptians instead!). And I have been appointed to the diplomatic party that is to go to Egypt to negotiate things.

So the question that burdens me is whether I can properly accept that appointment. I have heard that you are not only opposed to people praying to the Masters. You are also opposed to any kind of negotiation with foreign powers that is designed to improve the nation's security or undergird its independence (if that's what you can call it).

From the prophet Hosea ben Beeri
To Ulam ben Micah:

> 7:8Ephraim among the peoples, he wastes away;
>> Ephraim has become a loaf not turned over.
> 9Strangers have consumed his energy,
>> and he has not acknowledged it.
> Yes, grey hair has spread over him,
>> and he has not acknowledged it.
> 10Israel's majesty avows against it,
>> but they haven't turned back to Yahweh
>>> their God,
>> they haven't sought him despite all this.

¹¹Ephraim has become like a simple pigeon,
  without sense.
They've called on Egypt,
  they've gone to Assyria.
¹²When they go,
  I shall spread my net over them.
Like a bird in the heavens, I shall bring
      them down;
  I shall correct them in accordance with the
    report of their assembly.
¹³Oh, these people, because they've strayed
    from me;
  destruction for them, because they've rebelled
    against me.
Whereas I'm the one who could redeem them,
  but they themselves have spoken lies about me.
¹⁴They haven't cried out to me in their heart,
  when they wail on their beds.
Over grain and new wine they quarrel;
  they turn against me.
¹⁵I myself corrected them, strengthened their arms,
  but they think up bad things against me.
¹⁶They turn back, not to the One on High;
  they've become like a false bow.
Their officials will fall by the sword
    because of the condemnation of their tongue
    (i.e., their jabbering in the country of Egypt).
    (7:8–16)

Background and Foreground

Hosea has no doubt of the context in which Ulam has to think about his personal dilemma. Ephraim alternates between Assyria and Egypt as a potential source of support; Hosea takes the same attitude to both of them. His political

challenge to Ephraim, which would seem politically impractical, is that Ephraim has to sort out its relationship with
Yahweh first. Then Yahweh will help it sort out the politics.
The Ephraimites cry out as a result of the terrible calamity
that they have been through, but they haven't cried out to
Yahweh. They eat and they drink and they quarrel (over the
right policy?), but they criticize the way Yahweh is letting
things happen to them rather than turning to him. Yahweh
was the one who had made them what they are, but they have
deliberately acted in a dire way in their relationship with him.
They are faithless. They will find that turning from Assyria to
Egypt simply means more trouble from a different direction.
The last lines do give Ulam some hints about his dilemma.
The people who engage in the negotiations in Egypt will lose
their lives (maybe no more, but no less than the people they
represent) as a result of the condemnation that their stupid
discussions involve them in.

A Letter to Hosea from Ahaz
ben Jotham, King of Judah

To my lord Hosea ben Beeri in Jerusalem:

Here in Jerusalem, we have mixed feelings about the horrific
time people have had in Ephraim from the Assyrians. You know
that I deeply resented the way King Pekah tried to lean on me to
join them in rebelling against the Assyrians, threatening to see I
got deposed or assassinated so I could be replaced by someone
who was under his thumb. And I knew the Ephraimites were
good at assassination. Isaiah exhorted me not to worry about
these threats and not to have anything to do with rebelling. I
wasn't sure I was convinced by his argument about trusting in
Yahweh, but politically it suited me to go along with it. Assyria

has changed a lot since Tiglath-pileser took charge over the past decades, and it seemed unlikely that little nations like Syria, Ephraim, and Judah could resist the might of Assyria. And I was right, wasn't I? And that's why you are here in Jerusalem. I'm glad you managed to escape.

Of course, the policy I decided on was that I would appeal to Assyria myself, which wasn't what Isaiah had in mind, and as a result he won't talk to me now. I guess I can't blame him. But now that you've come to Jerusalem, it has raised more sharply the question whether your message to Ephraim applies to us in Judah. There are some things in that message that we are not afraid about. We don't go in for praying to deities other than Yahweh in the way the Ephraimites do. We don't have our own new-fangled sanctuaries and our own line of kings (or rather, lines of kings). We have Jerusalem as the city that Yahweh actually chose, and I am privileged to sit on the throne of David, whose line Yahweh established and to whose line he made a commitment. Does that mean we are safe? I can never get clear whether Isaiah thinks we are or not.

From the prophet Hosea ben Beeri in Jerusalem for Samaria
To His Majesty Ahaz ben Jotham King of Judah:

> 5:5bIsrael and Ephraim will collapse through their
> waywardness
> (Judah has fallen with them, too). (5:5b)

> 5:12I myself am like a moth to Ephraim,
> like rot to Judah's household. . . .
> 14Because I shall be like a lion to Ephraim,
> like a cougar to Judah's household. (5:12, 14)

> 6:4What shall I do with you, Ephraim,
> what am I to do with you, Judah,

When your commitment is like morning cloud,
    like dew going early? (6:4)

6:10bIsrael has become defiled 11a(Judah, too);
    he's appointed a harvest for you. (6:10b–11a)

8:14Israel has put out of mind its maker
    and built palaces,
    (and Judah has built many fortified towns).
I shall send off fire to its towns
    and it will consume its citadels. (8:14)

11:12Ephraim has surrounded me with lying,
    Israel's household with deceit.
(Judah still wanders with God,
    keeps faith with the sacred ones.) . . .
12:2Yahweh will argue with Judah,
    and attend to Jacob in accordance with
        his ways;
    in accordance with his practices he will give
        back to him. (11:12; 12:2)

1:7(But on Judah's household I will have compassion, and I will deliver them through Yahweh their God—I shall not deliver them through bow, through sword and through battle, through horses and through cavalry.) . . . 11The Judahites and the Israelites will collect together and make one head for themselves. They will go up from the country, because Jezreel's day will be great. (1:7, 11)

Background and Foreground

The prospect of the Ephraimite and Syrian kings' "visit" to Jerusalem caused understandable panic (see Isaiah 7). We don't know that Hosea himself moved to Jerusalem before or after the fall of Samaria, but the scroll recording his messages did find its way there, and it incorporates many notes that make clear that his message applies to Judah. Some of the references to Judah may have been aspects of his own preaching over the years. They might simply provide Ephraim with insights on how Yahweh looked at Ephraim's brother nation. Others look more like additional notes urging Judah to learn from Ephraim's mistakes. Yahweh promises that both peoples will make pilgrimage together when the time of restoration comes. Given the way relationships were between them, it is quite a promise.

Another Letter to Hosea from Ulam ben Micah in Egypt

To my lord Hosea ben Beeri in Jerusalem:

I don't know if you will remember that I wrote to you some years ago when I was appointed to an Ephraimite delegation in Egypt. I am now simply an Ephraimite who evaded becoming a forced migrant in Assyria and managed to escape to Egypt. I did listen to you in Samaria, and I realized that you were right in your critique of Ephraim, but I was too scared to stand up and be counted about it. We succeeded in getting a promise of Egyptian support, but it didn't do us any good when Shalmaneser invaded. Eventually Samaria fell and many people did get taken off as forced migrants. But when the fall looked inevitable, it seemed stupid to wait for it to happen— especially if you were tainted by association with Hoshea, as I was. So I joined the people who got out before it was too late, not to Judah or Ammon or somewhere like that, but to Egypt, because I'd been here and even had one or two contacts. So here I am in Migdol. But I'll never be at home here in Egypt. So the question that burdens me is whether Yahweh is finally finished with us. What do you think?

I've heard news from Judahite couriers that you yourself have taken refuge in Jerusalem and have been welcomed by King Ahaz, on the basis of not being identified with King Pekah who tried to lean on him to join an alliance with the Syrians. So I am sending this message in a diplomatic bag with the court correspondence in the hope that it will find you.

From the prophet Hosea ben Beeri in Jerusalem
To Ulam ben Micah in Migdol:

> 14:1Turn back, Israel,
> to Yahweh your God,
> because you've fallen through your
> waywardness.
> 2Take words with you,
> and turn back to Yahweh;
> Say to him, 'Will you carry it all, the
> waywardness?—
> receive something good: for bulls we'll make
> up with our lips.
> 3Assyria isn't to deliver us,
> we won't ride on horses.
> We will no more say "our God"
> to something made by our hands,
> because in you the orphan will find
> compassion.'
>
> 4I shall heal their turning away, I shall love them freely,
> because my anger has turned back from me.
> 5I shall become like dew to Israel;
> it will flourish like the lily.
> It will strike roots like the Lebanon;

⁶its shoots will grow.
Its splendour will be like an olive tree,
        its fragrance like the Lebanon.
⁷People who sit in its shade will again bring grain
                to life,
        and flourish like the vine,
        its fame like Lebanon wine.

⁸Ephraim:
'What shall I have to do with idols anymore?—
        I myself have answered and looked to him.
I myself am like a verdant juniper'—
        from me your fruit appears.

⁹Who is smart and discerning about these things,
        is discerning and acknowledges them?
Because Yahweh's ways are straight,
        and the faithful walk in them,
        but rebels collapse by them. (14:1–9)

Background and Foreground

It's a common pattern in the Prophets that Yahweh threatens a devastation that looks final if people do not turn back to him, but then after the devastation speaks of restoration. The last chapter of Hosea illustrates the pattern. The question it raises is whether *now*, at last, Ephraim will see sense and turn. There is no actual nation of Ephraim to do the turning. The nation as such no longer exists. But there are Ephraimites in Judah and elsewhere who might, and Ulam would be one of them. The next-to-last verse is a conversational exchange into which Hosea invites Ephraim; it imagines Ephraim at last turning, and Yahweh responding. The very last verse urges subsequent students of the Hosea scroll to see how it applies to them.

LETTERS TO JOEL

J oel doesn't give us concrete information about his date or background. He doesn't refer to any kings or to peoples such as the Assyrians or Babylonians. One clue he does give is that he uses expressions that also come in many of the other prophets, which suggests that he lived late enough in Israel's history to have been in a position to be closely familiar with their messages. So he might have been a contemporary of Malachi.

A Letter to Joel from Amnon ben Elijah in Jericho

To my lord Joel ben Pethuel in Jerusalem:

I send this letter to you from Jericho, in light of worrying news we have received from passing merchants. Our city is on one of the main routes from Arabia to Syria and Mesopotamia, and caravans of merchants often stay overnight here. The worrying news is that they tell of locust swarms infesting oases in Arabia. The locusts have apparently migrated from Africa and have been devastating such trees and crops as grow in that desert area. And we know that when the winds come from the south, the locusts also find their way toward us, up the Arabah from the Red Sea. Heavy rain will then encourage them to breed, or will mean that their eggs are more likely to hatch and develop into actual insects rather than dying. Of course, we don't usually get heavy rain down here in Jericho, which isn't a problem because we have the springs and the River Jordan, but this winter we have had good rains. At least, we thought they were good rains.

We have had small-scale locust infestations in the past, so we know a little of what a locust epidemic could be like. Spring is the time they usually come, and spring will soon be here. There seem to be locusts that instinctively target trees, and others that especially like wheat and barley and animal fodder, but they will also eat legumes and vegetables and the patches of fodder in the wilderness that are vital for our sheep.

Our people have developed ways of trying to control them. We can light fires and we can shout at them and try to chase them away, and we can get our children to shout at them and chase them. Actually, though, it can be scary for the children. And when the locusts come in serious numbers, they are impossible to control. It's like a giant black cloud. You can't see the sun. They can cover the land with their yellow bodies as far as the eye can see. They make a loud noise like an audience clapping. And they just eat up the grapes and the dates and the figs and the olives and the mulberries and the pomegranates and the nuts. Indeed, they don't just eat the fruit. They eat the foliage. And it's then doubtful if the trees will ever recover.

A locust epidemic could mean we end up with no grain to make bread and no fodder for the animals. It would mean a famine. Hundreds of people would die because they have nothing to eat. And it won't just be here in Jericho, because they will find their way up to Jerusalem.

So what should we do?

From the prophet Joel ben Pethuel in Jerusalem
To Amnon ben Elijah in Jericho:

> [2:1]Blow a horn in Zion,
>   sound out on my sacred mountain.
> All the country's inhabitants are to tremble,
>   because Yahweh's Day has come, because
>   it's near,
> [2q]A day of darkness and gloom,
>   a day of cloud and murk. . . .
>
> [12]But even now (Yahweh's declaration),
>   turn back to me with your whole heart,
>   with fasting, with crying, and with lamenting.
> [13]Tear your mind, not your clothes,
>   and turn back to Yahweh your God,
> Because he is gracious and compassionate,
>   long-tempered and vast in commitment,
>   and he relents of dealing badly.
> [14]Who knows, he may turn back and relent,
>   and let a blessing remain behind him,
>   an offering and a libation for Yahweh
>   your God?
>
> [15]Blow the horn in Zion,
>   declare a sacred fast, call an assembly.
> [16]Gather the people, make the congregation
>   sacred,
>   collect the elders.
> Gather the babies
>   and those nursing at the breast.
> The groom is to go out of his room,
>   the bride out of her tent.

¹⁷Between the porch and the altar
    the priests, Yahweh's ministers, are to cry.
They're to say, 'Spare your people, Yahweh,
    don't give your domain to reviling,
    as a byword against them for the nations.
Why should they say among the peoples,
    "Where is their God?"' (2:1–2a, 12–17)

Background and Foreground

Prophets often picture a coming disaster as if it is already happening or has actually happened. Speaking that way brings the threatened reality home to people and drives them to turn to God now. Amos came from a town not far from Jericho, and Joel is like Amos in wanting people to turn to Yahweh in light of the threat constituted by Yahweh's Day (see Amos 5:14–24), which they both say is coming in the form of an imminent catastrophe. Amos said it was going to be a day of disaster, a dark day. In Joel, it's going to be the locust epidemic. But unlike Amos, Joel doesn't say that the imminent disaster is an act of punishment for people's wrongdoing, and therefore he doesn't quite say that they need to repent. He does say that they need to turn to Yahweh. He encourages them to do so because of a theme he has in common with Jonah. It's a conviction going back to the Sinai story, that Yahweh "is gracious and compassionate, long-tempered and vast in commitment, and relenting of dealing badly" (Joel 2:13; compare Exodus 32:11–14; 34:6–7).

The parallel with Jonah continues with the "who knows" that follows (Joel 2:14; see Jonah 3:9): "Who knows, he may turn back and relent." Joel recognizes that prayer is properly confident, in the boldness with which it comes to Yahweh, but that it is also properly deferential. You don't take an answer for granted. The image of Yahweh letting a blessing remain behind him is distinctive to Joel, and it is telling in the context. It implies saying to Yahweh: "At least don't let the locusts destroy everything. Let there be something left." If Yahweh does, there is the possibility of future blessing—that is, future fruitfulness. And if there is something left and then there is a future blessing, there will be the wherewithal for an offering. It is a clever argument to use to Yahweh! Another clever argument follows: You don't want the nations to ask, tauntingly, "Where is their God," do you? It's an argument Joel takes up from the Psalms.

A Follow-Up to Joel from Amnon ben Elijah

To my lord Joel ben Pethuel in Jerusalem:

By now you know that the locusts have done their work here. Some of us acted as you said. When the Jerusalem priests proclaimed a fast and called for a prayer gathering at the temple, some of us came, but other people thought that it wasn't going to make a difference and that it was more important to be taking what practical measures we could to stem the locust tide.

When the locusts came, they were like an invading army, as disciplined as the Babylonians. You know how an army has people with different jobs? It was as if the locusts were like that. There were cutters and swarmers and devourers and exterminators. They were like miniature lions, with teeth just as sharp and effective. And they ate up the country like an army, like a force of war chariots with a corps of horses.

My grandfather, who lived in Jerusalem, told me that when Nebuchadnezzar's army invaded the country, they simply consumed it. It's always the way with an army. They couldn't bring all the supplies they needed from Babylon. They just assumed they would use ours. They requisitioned our grain stores and our oil and our wine, and as time went by during the siege of Jerusalem, they stripped our trees of olives and grapes and figs and pomegranates. This locust army did the same. They ate everything in their path. They'd consume everything in one field and then move on to the next. It was horrific. We tried to chase them off, but it didn't work. My grandfather told me about the way the Babylonian soldiers eventually took control of the city. There were people whose homes were set into the city wall with windows that faced out, so they blocked up the windows to stop the soldiers getting in, but the soldiers scrambled up the wall and hacked their way into the houses. These locusts were the same. We tried to seal any opening to the outside, but they scaled our walls and found their way into the house on the assumption that there might be food there. They were as agile as the fittest special forces.

And the result is devastation. You know how Jericho has been likened to the garden of Eden, compared with the desolate wilderness around? There were the date palms, and things grew so well here because it's warm and we have plenty of water. It's like a desolate wilderness now. It's as if there has been a fire that has raged through the region. You reminded us of how Amos told people to beware of the Day of Yahweh. People thought that the Day of Yahweh was going to be a time of great blessing, but he said it was going to be a day of catastrophe. And that's what this disaster has been like. It's been like the Day of Yahweh arriving.

From the prophet Joel ben Pethuel
To Amnon ben Elijah in Jericho:

> 2:18So Yahweh became passionate about his country,
>   and took pity on his people.
> 19Yahweh answered,
>   and said to his people,
> 'Here I am, I'm going to send grain to you,
>   new wine and fresh oil—you'll be full of it.
> I shall not ever again give you over
>   as an object of reviling among the nations.

²⁰I shall put the northerner far from you,
  thrust him into a dry and desolate country,
His face to the eastern sea,
  his rear to the western sea.
His smell will go up, his stench go up,
  because he has acted big. . . .

²³Members of Zion, celebrate,
  rejoice in Yahweh your God.
Because he's given you
  the autumn rain in faithfulness.
He's made rain come down for you,
  autumn rain and spring rain as before.
²⁴Threshing-floors will be full of grain,
  presses will abound in new wine and fresh oil.
²⁵I shall make good to you for the years
  that the locust and the grub have consumed,
The hopper and the cutter, my big force,
  which I sent off against you.
²⁶You will eat and eat and be full,
  and praise the name of Yahweh your God,
The one who acted in an extraordinary way
      with you;
    my people won't be ashamed permanently,
      and you will acknowledge it.
²⁷Because I will be within Israel,
  and I am Yahweh your God.
And there is no other,
  and my people will not be ashamed,
    permanently.

²⁸After that, I shall pour my breath on all flesh,
  and your sons and your daughters will
      prophesy.

> Your elderly will have dreams,
>   your young men will see visions.
>   ²⁹I shall also pour my breath
>   on servants and maidservants in those days.
>   (2:18–20, 23–29)

Background and Foreground

As prophets can picture a coming catastrophe as if it has already happened, they can picture the coming restoration and blessing as if it had already happened. The aim is parallel—to encourage people, to give them hope as they themselves picture what the prophet describes. They can see it as something that's so certain, it's as if it has already come about. Maybe the fact that the people of Judah recognized Joel's message as having come from Yahweh and let it find a place in their Scriptures indicates both that something like the epidemic happened and also that something like the blessing happened, though we don't have any record of either. Yahweh's driving the northerner far away fits with the picture of the locusts as a vast army. Armies usually arrive from the north. So the north comes to suggest the location of dark and threatening forces, the embodiment of something demonic. But the military imagery in Joel may mean that not only is an army an image for a locust horde; the locust horde can be an image for an army. Either way, Yahweh promises a time of relief and restoration. Fury has poured out on Joel's people in his visions, but Yahweh also speaks of another kind of pouring out.

Another Letter to Joel from Amnon ben Elijah

To my lord Joel ben Pethuel in Jerusalem:

It's fantastic to see the dates maturing on the palm trees again and the boys getting ready to shin up the trees to pick them,

and to see the olives and the grapes and the figs and the pomegranates, which are easier for grown-ups to harvest! It's almost
as if Yahweh's Day has arrived in the good sense. We had originally thought of Yahweh's Day as a day of great blessing, a day
when Yahweh delivered us from oppression and made our life
great, and you told us we had to see it as a day of disaster, as
Amos said it was going to be a dark day. And he was obviously
right. In his time, catastrophe came on Ephraim in the form
of the Assyrians, and then it came on Judah in the form of the
Babylonians—not to say the Edomites and the Ammonites and
the Moabites. . . . And the way you talked about the locusts
fitted this way of speaking. They were Yahweh's Day arriving,
you said. And when they came, it exactly fitted that. But now
that things have started to flourish again down here in God's
garden, it almost makes me think that Yahweh's Day in the
good sense has arrived.

So I suppose the question I want to ask you is, what is
Yahweh's Day, really? The question is not just about nature
but about politics. I mentioned to you the way my grandfather
used to talk about Nebuchadnezzar's army, and at least they
got what they deserved, but the Persians aren't really much of
an improvement. We're still part of somebody's empire. We're
not free. We still have to pay imperial taxes. Sometime, will
there be a Yahweh's Day that means we are free?

I'm sorry to trouble you again, but we don't have any
prophets down here in Jericho!

From the prophet Joel ben Pethuel
To Amnon ben Elijah in Jericho:

> $^{2:30}$I shall put portents in the heavens and in the earth,
>   blood, fire, and columns of smoke.
> ^{31}The sun will turn to darkness,
>   the moon to blood,

Before Yahweh's Day comes,
     great, extraordinary.
32aBut anyone who calls
     in Yahweh's name will escape . . .

3:2I shall collect all the nations
     and get them down to Jehoshaphat ['Yahweh
          has exercised authority'] Vale.
I shall enter into the exercise of authority with
          them there
     over my people, my domain, Israel,
     whom they scattered among the nations.
They shared out my country,
     3and for my people they cast the lot.
They gave a boy for a whore,
     sold a girl for wine and drank it.

9aCall out this among the nations,
     declare a sacred battle. . . .
10aBeat your hoes into swords,
     your pruning hooks into spears; . . .
12The nations are to stir themselves and go up
     to Jehoshaphat Vale,
Because there I shall sit to exercise authority
     over all the nations around.
13Put out the sickle,
     because the harvest has ripened.
Come, tread,
     because the vat is full.
The presses abound,
     because their bad dealing is great. . . .
17You will acknowledge that I am Yahweh,
     your God who dwells on Zion, my sacred
          mountain.

Jerusalem will be sacred;
    strangers will no more pass through it.
[18]On that day
    the mountains will drop sweet wine,
The hills will run with milk,
    all Judah's canyons will run with water.
A fountain will go out of Yahweh's house
    and water Acacias Wadi.
              (2:30–32a; 3:2–3, 9a, 10a, 12–13, 17–18)

Background and Foreground

The locust epidemic and the restoration of the land were *a* Day of Yahweh, but they invite people to look forward to *the* Day of Yahweh. Whereas people knew it would be a day when people were able to turn weapons of war into farming implements, in the meantime Joel mischievously turns that idea on its head. The nations are encouraged to turn their farming implements into weapons, but it's an ironic encouragement, because it won't get them anywhere in the battle that Yahweh wages against them! You can't find Yahweh-Has-Exercised Authority Vale on a map—it's a symbolic name devised in connection with the fact that Yahweh is going to exercise authority over nations that have raped and pillaged and enslaved. The point about the picture of Jerusalem being sacred and purified from strangers isn't that there will be only Israelites there but that it won't be spoiled by aggressors. Acacias was the name of a place across the Jordan from Jericho; Acacias Wadi is then another symbolic name. Acacias are trees that grow in the desert. A mere wadi (that is, a riverbed that only sometimes has water in it), with mere acacias in it, would contrast with Jericho, which had the springs that made it fertile. Yahweh's action "on that day" will transform nature and transform people.

LETTERS TO AMOS

Amos was a sheep breeder from Judah whom Yahweh commissioned to go and preach in Ephraim—in other words, in a foreign country. Amos himself usually refers to the country as Israel, its regular political title, so that by Israel he usually means just that northern nation, not "the people of Israel" as a whole; I will continue referring to it as Ephraim. Like Hosea, he was working during the last decades of Ephraim's life, maybe from the 760s BC onwards and thus starting slightly earlier than Hosea. He would then be the first prophet to have a collection of prophecies named after him. The prophecies presumably date from a time over some decades, like Hosea's, and they needn't be in chronological order in the scroll. Amos often refers to the city of Samaria, the capital of Ephraim, where it looks as if Hosea mostly preached. But Samaria's main sanctuary is at Beth-El, two days journey to the south, and it seems to be there that Amos preached.

Like Hosea, Amos preaches to a people who know that Yahweh is a God of love and mercy. In the worship at Beth-El they would sing psalms about Yahweh being one who blesses (for example, Psalms 29 and 67). They have known the success and prosperity of the reign of Jeroboam and the fulfillment of Yahweh's promise through Jonah (2 Kings 14:23–29), to which there is a reference in one of the imaginary letters. And they would be looking forward to "Yahweh's Day" as the time when that blessing will reach its fullest. Amos knows they are in danger of experiencing a different side of Yahweh and a different kind of day.

A Letter to Amos from Shema ben Malchiah, Aide to King Jeroboam

To my lord Amos in Beth-El:

I think you will know my name; you will see that this letter is impressed with my seal that has the picture of a roaring lion and identifies me as an aide of King Jeroboam. His majesty has been pleased to hear of your move to Ephraim from Judah. He prays that your staff are giving good oversight to your sheep business in Tekoa and that you will enjoy the cooler weather in Beth-El.

Here in Samaria it can seem as if we are at the center of the world, and it is in this connection that the king writes to you. We are at the center of a region that stretches from the Mediterranean on the west to the desert on the east, and from Mount Hermon in the north to the desert in the south. We are at a great crossroads between northeast and southwest. News reaches us quickly. And his majesty the king is burdened about things that are happening in the region. He wonders whether there is any word from Yahweh about them.

Some of these events are atrocities of which Ephraim has been the victim. You will know that there have long been tensions between us and our Syrian neighbors to the northeast, and these tensions have sometimes flared into actual fighting. A little while ago, his majesty's subjects across the Jordan were the victims of aggression from Syria. King Hazael ben Hadad marched south from Damascus into that area that was geographically vulnerable to the Syrians, and it was as if they threshed the country with threshing sleds that had iron spikes in the bottom. The result was that the people of Gilead totally lost their freedom; they were turned into serfs of Hazael. But there are signs that the Syrians are not as strong as they once were, and his majesty has plans to do something about it. That fact makes him all the more concerned to know what Yahweh thinks about the situation and whether he would have Yahweh's support.

Other events in the region have nothing to do with Ephraim, but it doesn't stop us from being concerned. You yourself will have heard about the Philistines being engaged in human trafficking. The people of Gaza captured the entire community from a village just across the border from them, transported them through southern Judah, and sold them as a conscript labor force to the Edomites. We ourselves know about other examples of the same thing. We were given a report about a camel train winding its way through Shechem, in between where you are and where I am, which was also on its way to Edom but was coming from Phoenicia to the northwest. Such camel trains are quite a common occurrence; we just collect transit taxes from the camel drivers and let them carry on their way. But this camel train was troublesome because the wares were human. It had come from Tyre, and it was also taking the inhabitants of an entire village to Edom for them to use as a conscript labor force. There was another aspect that made it a deeper atrocity. There had been a treaty relationship between these people and the Phoenicians, which meant that the Phoenicians had agreed to relate to them as if they were all one people, almost members of the same family. But they just ignored the treaty obligation. How can international relations proceed if people just tear up their commitments in this way?

From the prophet Amos in Beth-El
To Shema ben Malchiah, aide to His Majesty King Jeroboam
in Samaria:

> 4:13Because there, one who shapes mountains,
> creates wind,
> Tells human beings what his thinking is,
> makes dawn into darkness,
> Treads on earth's high places—
> Yahweh, God of Armies, is his name. (4:13)

> 5:7You who turn the exercise of authority to poison
> and set down faithfulness on the earth!
> 8He's the one who makes Pleiades and Orion,
> turns deep darkness to dawn.
> He darkens day into night,
> the one who calls the water of the sea,
> Pours it out on the face of the earth—
> Yahweh is his name—
> 9The one who flashes destruction on the vigorous,
> so that destruction comes on the fortification.
> (5:7–9)

> 9:5The Lord Yahweh of Armies—
> he touches the earth and it melts,
> and all the people who live in it mourn.
> All of it rises like the Nile,
> and sinks like Egypt's Nile.
> 6He built his lofts in the heavens,
> and founded his structure on the earth,
> The one who calls to the sea's water
> and pours it over the face of the earth—
> Yahweh is his name. (9:5–6)

Background and Foreground

Shema's name appears on a seal made of jasper found at Megiddo in Israel in the 1900s; Megiddo was an important town guarding a key pass through the mountains twenty or so miles north of Samaria. The seal subsequently disappeared while it was on its way to the Istanbul museum, but fortunately someone had made an impression of it in bronze. At the top of the seal is the name Shema, in the middle the picture of a roaring lion, and at the bottom the words "Servant of Jeroboam."

In these three declarations about Yahweh, Amos affirms that Yahweh's worldwide, cosmic power means that no nation can assume it will get away with wrongdoing. The three descriptions of Yahweh come from different points in the Amos scroll, but they have this common theme concerning Yahweh's power, with a common implication. People have to deal with "Yahweh of Armies"—that is, the God who has all power at his control. Amos includes only one phrase to describe the wrongdoing that people are guilty of: they are involved in turning the exercise of authority to poison and putting faithfulness to rest. Amos thus uses two expressions that are a key pair in the First Testament: the exercise of authority or government or rule or decision-making power, and the exercise of faithfulness and truthfulness to people (the usual translation is justice and righteousness). The two—the exercise of power and the exercise of faithfulness—are supposed to belong together. They express the essence of what social justice means in the First Testament. Amos neatly articulates the scandalous way in which the faithful exercise of power can be thwarted and the danger the nations are risking. His words could form an interim response to the letter Shema brought from his boss. But it will turn out in a moment that Amos has something more pointed to say in response to that report from the king about the Syrians, the Philistines, and the Tyrians.

A Follow-Up to Amos from Shema ben Malchiah, Aide to King Jeroboam

To my lord Amos in Beth-El:

His majesty thanks you for your affirmations of Yahweh's opposition to the kind of activities he described in his letter. But he is not sure of the answer to his practical question. What, if anything, should he be doing about such atrocities? In order to underline the question, he draws your attention to some further examples.

There are the Edomites themselves. Again, you know about this. They are a problem to Judah, as Syria is a problem to Ephraim—they are the neighbors with whom there are often disputes about territory. It's morally trickier because the Edomites are descended from Esau, from Jacob's brother, so we are all really family. But the Edomites have been quite happy to wield the sword against Judah in a way that generated atrocities. You might have thought that they would have some fellow feeling with Judah as people who ultimately came from the same womb, some compassion for Judah. But it's not the case.

Further, there are the Ammonites. Across the Jordan again from us, they have also been campaigning in Gilead to their north. They have been guilty of the worst war crime, though I know it is the kind of thing that armies have often done. They made a point of slaying women who they could see were pregnant. They weren't just interested in killing people in general in the population, as well as killing the men they were fighting; they made a point of driving their swords through these women's bellies. They wanted not just to put down this generation of people in Gilead but to make sure there wouldn't be another generation, so they could be sure of taking over their land for themselves.

After that, the action of the Moabites across the Jordan from you may seem trivial. The Moabites are also neighbors of the Edomites. You know, and you can tell from things that I have said already, that the Edomites are happy to be at war with anyone. And the Moabites wanted to think up something they could do to get their own back for when the Edomites have fought them. So they sent a raiding party into Edom and commissioned it to go for the royal tombs. The Edomite kings of course were interred in impressive rock tombs in the rugged Edomite terrain. But the thing about a rock tomb is that it's also not hard to get into. So the Moabites killed the tomb guards and pushed the boulder aside that was sealing the tomb to protect the body of the king who had died most recently. They got the body out, took it back to Moab, and ceremonially burned it. One has to have some sympathy even for an Edomite king. He wants to be able to rest in peace. But they wouldn't let him. They treated his remains as if they were just what was left of an animal.

Now the Syrians and the Philistines and the Phoenicians and the Edomites and the Ammonites and the Moabites don't have the Torah, but they don't need to have read the Torah in order to know that the kind of things they have been doing are wrong. Anybody who hasn't just hardened their conscience knows it. His majesty also knows that the Judahites are lax in their attitude to the Torah, and he guesses that this is one reason why my lord Amos has left Judah and come to settle in Ephraim.

So the policies of these nations raise various questions for his majesty. Should he write in protest to the authorities in these nations? Should he cut off diplomatic relations with them? Should he cancel treaties with them? Should he terminate trading relations? Should he attack them on Yahweh's behalf? Clearly some of these decisions would be risky and costly. But his majesty doesn't feel he can simply turn a blind eye to what amounts

to rebellion after rebellion against what they should know are
God's expectations—three rebellions, four rebellions. . . . Would
Yahweh turn back the punishment of such actions?

From the prophet Amos in Beth-El
To Shema ben Malchiah, aide to His Majesty King Jeroboam
in Samaria:

    2:6 Yahweh has said this:

> For three rebellions by Israel,
>   for four I shall not turn it back,
> Because of their selling a faithful person for silver,
>   a needy person for a pair of boots.
> 7 You who trample the head of poor people into
>   the earth of the ground,
>   and twist the way of humble people!
> An individual and his father go to a girl,
>   in order to treat my sacred name as ordinary.
> 8 On garments given in pledge
>   they lie down by every altar.
> In their God's house they drink
>   the wine of people who have been defrauded.

> 9 And I'm the one who annihilated the Amorite before
>   them,
>   whose height was like the height of cedars,
>   and who was as sturdy as oaks.
> I annihilated his fruit above
>   and his roots below.
> 10 And I'm the one who took you up
>   from the country of Egypt.
> I enabled you to go through the wilderness for
>   forty years,

to take possession of the Amorite's country.
¹¹I raised up prophets from your children,
    consecrated people from your young men.
It is indeed so, isn't it, Israelites (Yahweh's
      declaration),
    ¹²but you made the consecrated people drink
      wine
    and you ordered the prophets, 'You will not
      prophesy.'

¹³There, I'm going to make a split beneath you as a cart
      makes a split
    when full of its grain.
¹⁴Flight will perish from the swift,
    the strong won't firm up his energy.
The strong man won't save his life,
    ¹⁵the one who wields the bow won't stand.
One swift on his feet won't save himself,
    one riding a horse won't save his life.
¹⁶The firmest of mind among the strong men
    will flee naked on that day (Yahweh's
      declaration). (2:6–16)

⁹:⁷You're like the Kushites [Sudanese]
    to me, Israelites, aren't you (Yahweh's
      declaration)?
I got Israel up from the country of Egypt,
    didn't I—
    and the Philistines from Kaphtor, and the
      Aramites [Syrians] from Qir?
⁸There, the Lord Yahweh's eyes
    are on the kingdom that does wrong;
I annihilate it
    from on the face of the earth. (9:7–8)

Background and Foreground

Both the king's imaginary letters were based on Amos 1:3–2:5. Here, Amos's message to the king is, in effect, put your own house in order before you think of critiquing other peoples. Ordinary people who get into economic trouble are the victims of people who can profit from them. Two men within a family can have sex with the same girl. Worshipers make use of resources that issue from taking advantage of needy people. If the God who had acted on the Israelites' behalf in the past sends people to challenge them, they prefer them to keep quiet. Yes, he did bring the Israelites from Egypt, but then he had been involved in the destinies of their neighbors, too. The question of whether he acts against a people is determined by their faithfulness or their wrongdoing, not his past relationship with them. And if he does act against his people, as he threatens, it has devastating and inescapable consequences.

A Letter to Amos from Amaziah ben Ahimaaz, Priest in Beth-El

To my lord Amos:

His majesty the king has received your letter and he is displeased that you had copies circulated in Samaria. It has caused controversy, disquiet, and unrest among the people of the city. He has written to me about you, and I am therefore writing to make the following points to you in this letter which I am also making the subject of public proclamation here.

First, you spoke as if Israel meant nothing special to Yahweh, yet you also referred to the fact that Yahweh entered into a relationship with Israel. It was a special relationship, not just with Ephraim but with the twelve clans of the original Israel, including Judah, from which we were forced to split because of the oppressive policies of David's grandson. We are the blessed beneficiaries of Yahweh's grace. Yahweh entered into a covenant relationship with us that was originally proclaimed here in our country at Shechem, halfway between where I am in Samaria and where you are in Beth-El. Israel was the only people Yahweh acknowledged in that way, out of all the peoples of the world. How could it be that Yahweh would contemplate annihilating us? Do you not believe that he is the God of love and grace and faithfulness? You know what the Psalms say about him. He is the God who gives and blesses. He is not a God who is angry and destructive. Your message is in conflict with the faith of Israel, with the Torah itself.

Second, what right do you have to be telling us what Yahweh is saying against Ephraim? Are you claiming that you walk alongside Yahweh and he shares things with you? Are you claiming to be like the town crier who issues proclamations to the people of the city? Do you really expect us to be afraid of what you see? Are you saying that Yahweh is like a lion who is attacking us? That he is like a hunter who is setting a trap for a bird? Is that the sort of person Yahweh is? We believe it's just your imagination. You're simply a Judahite agent sent to demoralize us. So if you will not take part in the worship at Beth-El in a reverent way without creating a disturbance and thereby making it impossible for other people to worship, then you should leave and get back to Judah where they will reward you for critiquing us.

From the prophet Amos in Beth-El
To Amaziah ben Ahimaaz, Priest in Beth-El:

> 3:1Listen to this word that Yahweh has spoken about you, Israelites, about the entire kin-group that I took up from Egypt:

²Only you did I acknowledge
    from all earth's kin-groups.
Therefore I shall attend to you
    for all your wayward acts.
³Do two walk together
    unless they've taken counsel?
⁴Does a lion roar in the forest
    and it has no prey?
Does a cougar give voice from its abode
    unless it has caught something?
⁵Does a bird fall in a trap on the earth
    and there's no snare there?
Does a trap come up from the ground
    and it hasn't actually caught something?
⁶If a horn sounds in a town,
    doesn't the people tremble?
And if something happens to a town,
    isn't it Yahweh who's acted?
⁷Because the Lord Yahweh does nothing
    except he has revealed his plan
    to his servants the prophets.

⁸A lion has roared,
    who would not be afraid?
The Lord Yahweh has spoken,
    who wouldn't prophesy? (3:1–8)

7:14a'I wasn't a prophet and I wasn't a prophet's son; rather I was a cattleman and a dresser of sycamore figs. ¹⁵But Yahweh took me from following the flock, and Yahweh said to me, "Go, prophesy to my people Israel."

¹⁶Now, listen to Yahweh's word. You're saying,

"You shouldn't prophesy against Israel. You shouldn't preach against Isaac's household." [17]Therefore Yahweh has said this: "Your wife will whore in the town. Your sons and your daughters will fall by the sword. Your land will be shared out by measuring line. You yourself will die on unclean land. Israel will go into exile, exile away from its land.' (7:14a–17).

Background and Foreground

"Yes," says Amos, "Your rhetorical questions are exactly what Yahweh is saying to you." Yahweh had indeed "acknowledged" Israel (Amos 3:2). Like Hosea, Amos uses the ordinary verb for "know," which means more than merely being aware of them (compare Hosea 5:3). As is the case with Hosea's talk of people "knowing" or "acknowledging" Yahweh (for example, Hosea 5:4), it means recognizing and choosing to make a commitment. But Yahweh's choice and commitment exposes Israel to Yahweh's discipline rather than implying it will escape that discipline.

"Things have causes, don't they?" Amos goes on. "You're going to experience some things that Yahweh will have caused, unless you start taking some notice of what I as your lookout say." He hardly implies that Yahweh causes every disaster that ever happens; after all, the opening questions about friends and lions and traps are not universal truths, and neither is the statement about Yahweh causing disasters. But when a prophet speaks and then things happen, people are wise to assume it's not a coincidence. And a prophet is speaking. He is speaking because Yahweh sent him, not because he was trained to be a prophet. Amaziah is taking a big risk in trying to shut him down.

Amos's last warning (7:17) will especially provoke Amaziah to reply in the letter that follows.

A Follow-Up to Amos from Amaziah ben Ahimaaz, Priest in Beth-El

To my lord Amos:

Don't you dare threaten me! And I am writing to his majesty the king to report your words about him, that "Jeroboam will die by the sword, Ephraim will go into exile, exile away from its soil." You should be wary of the consequences.

Beth-El is one of our two national cathedrals, and because it's here in the south of the country, nearer the capital, it's the more important of the two. It's where the people of Ephraim gather to worship the God of Israel and to pray for his blessing upon us as a people. It's where the king comes for the festivals. The altar here was first set up by our ancestor Abraham. Yahweh appeared to Jacob here when Isaac sent him off to find a wife. When Israel settled in the promised land, Joseph's two sons' clans settled in the area covered by Samaria and Beth-El. Beth-El was a holy place way before anyone had heard of Jerusalem. You have no right to be dismissive of it.

For me it's a privilege to chant out the invitation to people to worship here: "Come to Beth-El, bring your sacrifices and your tithes, your thank offerings and your love offerings." It's a wonder to watch people celebrating the festivals and bringing their grain offerings and their burnt offerings. It's a marvel to listen to the sanctuary choir singing their praise songs and to listen to the music sounding out. You have no right to be so dismissive of people's sincere, heartfelt worship.

From the prophet Amos in Beth-El
To Amaziah ben Ahimaaz, priest in Beth-El:

4:2aThe Lord Yahweh has sworn by his sacredness: . . .

⁴Come to Beth-El and rebel—
    to Gilgal, multiply the rebelling.
Bring your sacrifices every morning,
    your tenths every three days.
⁵Burn your thank offering of leavened bread,
    call out voluntary offerings, make them heard,
    because so you love it, Israelites (the Lord
        Yahweh's declaration). (4:2a, 4–5)

⁵:⁴ᵇEnquire of me, and live,
    ⁵don't enquire of Beth-El,
Don't go to Gilgal,
    don't cross over to Beer-Sheba.
Because Gilgal is definitely to go into exile,
    and Beth-El is to become nothing.
⁶Enquire of Yahweh and live,
    so he doesn't break out like fire
On Joseph's household, and consume,
    and there's no one to quench it for Beth-El.
      (5:4b–6)

⁵:²¹I've been hostile, I've rejected your festivals;
    I don't savour your assemblies.
²²Even when you offer me burnt offerings,
    and your grain offerings, I shall not
      accept them.
To a fellowship offering of well-fed animals
    I shall not look.
²³Remove from me the noise of your songs;
    I shall not listen to the music of your
      mandolins.
²⁴The exercise of authority is to roll like water,
    faithfulness like a perennial wadi.

²⁵Was it sacrifices and an offering that you
     presented to me
in the wilderness for forty years,
    household of Israel? (5:21–25)

Background and Foreground

Amos issues two exhortations to the people of Ephraim. He is the great master of rhetoric in the First Testament (not bad for a sheep breeder), and the two exhortations are superficially contradictory but make the same point. Yes, go and take part in the great worship festivals. I know you find them spiritually encouraging. Oh, there's this snag. Actually, they are acts of rebellion against Yahweh. Or alternatively: whatever you do, don't go to the great worship festivals. I know you find them spiritually encouraging. But when you go to them, you are ignoring the fact that disaster is coming. You think you are in touch with Yahweh when you go to the festivals. Actually, you aren't. He doesn't go. If you want to talk to him, talk to him, but he's not there.

And what he wants is for you to ask about the way power is exercised with faithfulness among you by the people who have power in government or business or education or worship, or rather about the way it isn't. When he speaks of power being exercised in a faithful way and compares it with a perennial wadi, the image might raise a wistful smile, because a wadi is pretty much by definition a stream that runs only when it's just rained. Power being exercised in a faithful way would be a similar miracle. Yahweh then speaks in hyperbole in his rhetorical question about sacrifices and offerings in the wilderness, speaking as if they didn't offer them at all there. The first expectations he expressed at Sinai, which came in the Ten Commandments, talk about faithfulness to Yahweh and to one another. The Torah does speak of sacrifices and offerings subsequently during the people's time in the wilderness, though those sacrifices and offerings would be on nothing like the scale of Beth-El or Dan or Jerusalem.

A Letter to Amos from Bered ben Shetulah of Shechem

To my lord Amos in Beth-El:

We're an ordinary family with an allocation of land near Shechem. The land is quite fertile, and the area usually gets a reasonable amount of rain. We have vines and olive groves and figs, and a few sheep and goats. We are better off in this respect than many people in tougher parts of Ephraim. We have been blessed.

But the last few years, things have been difficult. It's now just after Passover, and my wife Rachel bat Jehoshaphat and I were talking about the situation in bed last night, which is why I am writing. We were talking quietly because my widowed sister-in-law and Rachel's orphan nephew were sleeping not far away (our son and his wife and the various little children were in the house next door). We were talking anxiously because it looks as if this year's harvest is going to be no better than last year's.

We've had a series of drought years, and the grain crop has been poor. We haven't had enough to mill and to bake enough bread for us to eat and be full, and therefore we haven't had enough to keep for next year, so that we can sow properly. Whereas in the past we've done better (thank God) than some other areas, in recent years it's been hard. Our well dried up, and our cistern never filled because it didn't rain enough, so we've had to walk miles to beg water from a village that was more fortunate. Other people like us have been struck with blight and mildew, so although things grew, they ended up with no more to eat than we had. And one year there was a locust epidemic that devastated the orchard and the olive grove. Our problems haven't been just in the realm of nature. We were subject to raids by Philistine gangs coming up from their area to the west, and some of the young men in Shechem got killed in the fighting.

We've asked ourselves whether we deserve what has been happening. We've prayed a lot about our situation. We try to live honest lives. We make our commitments, and we back them up with an oath in the name of the great image of Yahweh in Beth-El, of which we have a small-scale local equivalent in our house. So Rachel suggested I should write to you. What do you think is going on? What is going to happen? What does the future hold?

From the prophet Amos in Beth-El
To Bered ben Shetulah of Shechem:

> 4:6Even though I—I have given you
> > emptiness of teeth in all your towns,
> Lack of food in all your places,
> > but you haven't turned back to me (Yahweh's
> > > declaration).
> 7Even though I—I have withheld the rain
> > from you
> > when it was still three months to the harvest.
> I'd let it rain on one town
> > but not let it rain on another town.
> One plot of land would be rained on,
> > but a plot on which it would not rain would
> > > wither.
> 8Two or three towns would wander
> > to another town to drink water.

But they wouldn't be full,
>but you haven't turned back to me (Yahweh's
>>declaration).

⁹I have struck you down with blight and with
>mildew,
>>multiplying it on your gardens and your
>>orchards.

The locust would eat your fig trees and olives,
>but you haven't turned back to me (Yahweh's
>>declaration).

¹⁰I sent off an epidemic among you
>in the manner of Egypt,

I killed your young men with the sword,
>with your captured horses,

Made the smell of your camps rise, even into your
>nostrils,
>>but you haven't turned back to me (Yahweh's
>>declaration). . . .

¹²Therefore this is what I shall do to you, Israel;
>because I shall do this to you,
>>get ready to meet your God, Israel. (4:6–12)

⁸:¹¹There, days are coming (a declaration of the Lord
>Yahweh)
>when I shall send famine through the
>>country—

Not famine of bread, not thirst for water,
>but rather of hearing Yahweh's words.

¹²People will wander from sea to sea
>and roam from north to east,

To seek Yahweh's word,
>but they won't find it.

¹³On that day beautiful girls and young men
>will faint with thirst.

¹⁴People who swear by the liability of Samaria,
    and say, 'As your god lives, Dan,'
    and 'As the way to Beer-Sheba lives,'
        will fall and not rise again. (8:11–14)

Background and Foreground

Bered sounds like a good man who wants to do his best for his family and sees himself as honoring Yahweh, but somehow things have gone wrong in his understanding of who Yahweh is. It's ironic that he lives near Shechem. Joshua 24 describes a key occasion when the requirements of the Torah were read out there for everyone to hear. It would be nice to imagine priests in Ephraim listening to the kind of message Amos has to give to Ephraim and to the way it will affect ordinary people. But solemnly, one of the consequences of people not listening to what Yahweh has to say is that he stops speaking. If people are addicted to swearing by the supposed gods imaged in the Ephraimite sanctuaries and praying to them, Yahweh may leave them to it.

A Letter to Amos from Shual ben Zophah of Beth-Imrin

To my lord Amos in Beth-El:

My family has been swindled out of its land near Samaria, and I have heard that you are concerned about that kind of thing, and I don't know if you can help us.

I say "swindled," but I'm not claiming that it was actually illegal. Our land was (is) near Beth-Imrin, an hour's walk from Samaria. It's on the east side of the mountain ridge, and the land isn't quite as good as the land on the ridge or to the west where there's more rain, but it's good enough, and it's our land,

and we love it. My family have looked after it for generations. I grew up there and I was involved in caring for it and pulling out weeds and climbing to the top of the olive trees to get the top olives from as young as I can remember. We could grow enough grain and we had an orchard and an olive grove. We used to take the surplus grain and figs and olives and grapes into Samaria and trade them for other things we needed, like pots and iron implements.

But we've had some tough years, and from our land we hadn't gotten enough produce for ourselves, let alone a surplus to trade with. So I took a job as an assistant to a metalworker in the town—I don't have any skills for that work, but I could do the laboring. And one of the farmers with land a bit further up the ridge that had been doing okay, a man named Heber ben Beriah—he lent my family seed for sowing. The land itself was the collateral; that's how things work. He wasn't exactly doing us a favor, and I'd heard about loan sharks and people losing their land in this way, and maybe I should have been suspicious, but he seemed a nice man and what alternative did we have?

So I took this job, and my sons carried on working the farm, and we hoped things would work out. But they didn't. There was another year when the rains didn't come. Again the harvest wasn't enough to feed us, let alone to give us enough to sow for the next year, let alone enough to trade with, let alone enough to pay back our debt. . . . And the pattern more or less repeated itself the next year, and Heber ben Beriah said he was going to take us to court in Beth-Imrin. So he gave me a day when I had to take time off work (that's another story) and appear with him in front of the elders in the town square in Beth-Imrin. It was horrible. The elders were my peers, of course—the other heads of households in the area. I was so ashamed. There was nobody else in the same position. Nobody else was doing really well, but they were managing.

I argued that the Torah gave people like me six years to

get out of trouble like this, but Heber ben Beriah insisted that
they shouldn't give me the benefit of that rule. He said there
was no prospect of me getting out of the mess we were in. To
tell you the truth, he was right, I'm not a very skilled farmer
any more than a skilled metalworker. As you can tell, I'm okay
at writing letters, but I'm not a Levite and I can't earn a living
as a scribe. Anyway, he argued that they should let someone
who knew more about farming take over the land. My family
could always continue as paid laborers. The other elders were
sympathetic to me, but they were too scared to decide in my
favor. So we lost our land, and now we're just peasants working land that belongs to someone else. We're working our own
land, but it doesn't belong to us now. And no matter how hard
we work, we're never going to get it back. I've ruined things for
my sons and their wives, and for their sons, as well as for me.
It'll probably mean that my grandsons will never be able to get
someone to marry them, because what father is going to let his
daughter marry a peasant? Or maybe they will end up taking
a job in the town like me.

It all seems unfair. What do you think? What does Yahweh
think?

From the prophet Amos in Beth-El
To Shual ben Zophah of Beth-Imrin and to King Jeroboam in
Samaria:

> 5:11Therefore, because you tax the poor person,
>   take a levy of grain from him:
> You've built houses of square stone,
>   but you won't live in them.
> 12Because I have got to know your many acts of
>   rebellion,
>   your numerous wrongdoings.
> You adversaries of the faithful, takers of a bribe,

who have turned aside the needy in the
gateway.

[13]Therefore the person of insight keeps silent at such a
time,
because it's a bad time.
[14]Enquire after what is good, not what is bad, in
order that you may live;
thus Yahweh, God of Armies, will be
with you,
as you've said.
[15]Be hostile to what is bad, be loyal to what
is good,
establish the exercise of authority in the
gateway.
Perhaps Yahweh, God of Armies, will be gracious
to what remains of Joseph. (5:11–15)

[6:4]You who lie on ivory beds,
lounging on their couches,
Eating lambs from the flock,
bullocks from within the stall,
[5]Making music to the sound of the mandolin like
David,
people who have composed for themselves on
musical instruments,
[6]Drink with bowls of wine,
anoint themselves with the finest oils,
but haven't got sick at the breaking of Joseph!
(6:4–6)

[8:4]Listen to this, you who trample the needy person,
who make the humble people in the country
cease,

⁵Saying, 'When will the new month be over,
  so we can sell wheat,
  and the sabbath, so we can lay out grain—
Making the barrel measure small but the
    sheqel big,
  falsifying the scales by deceit,
⁶Acquiring the poor people for silver,
  the needy person for a pair of boots,
  and selling sweepings as grain?'
⁷Yahweh has sworn by the Majesty of Jacob,
  'If I ever put out of mind any of their
    doings . . .' (8:4–7)

Background and Foreground

Shual is more unfortunate than Bered in the way things have been turning out on his land, and more unfortunate in the consequences. The process he describes is one whereby a farmer who is more fortunate or more skilled or more hard-working can take advantage of someone who is unfortunate or less skilled or lazy. It may involve dishonesty. But it need not; it can simply mean making the system work to your advantage. The challenge to the people with power in the community is to use their power in a good way. Otherwise, in the end there will be terrible trouble, even for the people who are doing okay at the moment.

A Letter to Amos from Ahi ben Abdiel in Gilead

To my lord Amos in Beth-El:

You know that King Jeroboam has had a triumphant time here in Gilead, east of the Jordan. In the time of his predecessors,

King Jehu and King Jehoahaz, the Syrians invaded Ephraim and took control of the entire country this side of the Jordan, the whole of Gilead and Bashan, the entire area belonging to the clans east of the Jordan—Gad and Reuben and the Manassites who lived this side of the river. It didn't mean we were thrown out of the country. It did mean we found ourselves under Syrian control and we had to pay Syrian taxes. But nowadays, the Syrians are nowhere near as strong. So King Jeroboam made up his mind that Ephraim should take back control of the area. He told us to pray for Yahweh to make it possible.

Some of us managed to get to the festival in Dan, not so far away, and the priest reminded us that the festival pointed to the great Day of Yahweh that will come one day, when Yahweh's promises of blessing will be fulfilled. And Jeroboam was encouraged by a promise Yahweh gave through a prophet called Jonah ben Amittay. In fact, Jeroboam conquered an area from the far north, Lebo Hamath, to Wadi Arabah in the far south, to the Dead Sea. He conquered places like Lo Debar south of Lake Galilee, in Gilead, and Karnaim, the most important town in the Bashan, on the way to Damascus.

So we've found ourselves part of Ephraim again, which is great. It was as if the Day of Yahweh actually had arrived. We had a fantastic festival of thanksgiving here in Gilead, and they had another one in Samaria. We made burnt offerings, sacrificing a whole animal and giving it all to Yahweh. We slaughtered an ox for the festival and offered some to Yahweh and feasted on some of it for ourselves. We sang and we rejoiced and we prayed.

But the puzzling thing is this. One could hardly complain at the way we lost that land in the time of King Jehu and King Jehoahaz. Neither of them were very good at living by Yahweh's expectations. The way they exercised government may have been efficient and effective, but it wasn't especially moral. It was almost poisonous. But frankly, King Jeroboam isn't very different (you'll destroy this letter when you've read it, won't you?). So it's a total surprise that Yahweh made that promise through Jonah and fulfilled it.

In another sense, it's not a surprise. We know that Yahweh is a merciful God and that he had not said that he would blot out Ephraim from under the heavens. Yet we also know that he doesn't just ignore what his people do. So my question is, what's going to happen now? They say that you stand in the succession of Jonah. You bring Yahweh's message like he did. So what is Yahweh's message?

From the prophet Amos in Beth-El
To Ahi ben Abdiel in Gilead:

> ^{5:18}Hey, you who wish
>   for Yahweh's Day.
> What good really is Yahweh's Day to you?—
>   it will be darkness, not light.
> ¹⁹As when someone flees from before a lion
>   and a bear meets him,
> Or he comes home,
>   leans his hand on a wall,
>   and a snake bites him.
> ²⁰Yahweh's Day will be darkness not light,
>   won't it,
>   gloom, with no brightness to it. (5:18–20)

> ^{8:10}I shall turn your festivals into mourning,
>   all your songs into lamenting.
> I shall put sack on all hips,
>   shornness on every head,
> I shall make it like the mourning for an only
>   child,
>   its end a truly bitter day. (8:10)

6:12Do horses run on a cliff,
> or does one plough it with cattle?
> Because you've turned the exercise of authority to
>> venom,
>   faithful fruit to poison,
> 13You who rejoice at No-Thing,
> who say 'It was by our strength, wasn't it,
> that we took Karnaim for ourselves?'
> 14Because here am I, about to raise up against you,
> Israel's household (a declaration of Yahweh,
>>   God of Armies)—
> A nation, and they'll afflict you
> from Lebo Hamath to Wadi Arabah.
>   (6:12–14)

Background and Foreground

The background to Amos's warning is that Yahweh's Day was a time people looked forward to as a time of ultimate blessing, as we noted in connection with Joel. Amos turns the idea upside down. It has to be a day of disaster, not joy. It would be a bitter day, not a festive one. When people gathered for worship, it would be for lamentation instead of praise. Amos would surely sound as if he is describing something that is against nature. The problem is that Samaria has turned the life of the nation into something that is against nature: government works for the benefit of the governors instead of the benefit of the governed. Amos has to confirm Ahi's suspicions about how Yahweh surely must take action against Ephraim, notwithstanding the grace he has been showing. Amos loves playing with words to make a point. One of the places Ahi ben Abdiel mentions is Lo Debar (at least, that's a spelling in 2 Samuel 9:4–5). But Amos spells it Lo Dabar, which would mean "No Thing." Jeroboam's conquests were really worth nothing.

A Letter to Amos from Makbiram bat Elimelek in Hazor

To my lord Amos in Beth-El:

My husband and I are concerned at rumors that are circulating up here in northern Ephraim about the messages you say come from Yahweh. We live in Hazor, north of Lake Galilee, which has a reputation for being the biggest town in Ephraim—a much more impressive place than Samaria. Hazor is a bit hot in the summer but it's lovely in the winter, and the king and the really wealthy people in Samaria like coming here for a winter break—some of them keep a holiday home here. And the town stands up a bit from the area around, partly because it's built on the ruins of earlier towns that have been here for centuries, so it gets the benefit of the breeze blowing from the west in the afternoons.

Hazor is not as big as it once was, but it's always been an important town because of where it's located, on the main road from the northeast to the southwest. Anyone traveling from Damascus to Jaffa or Gaza or Egypt is probably going to come this way. In wartime armies come this way, and in peacetime merchants do. My husband Elmattan is one of them. He has a shipping business that transports cloth and jewelry from Damascus to those places to the southwest and to Samaria. That's how we came to hear the rumors, because he was away in Samaria on business and the town was full of talk about you and your preaching at the sanctuary in Beth-El and about the king's worries about it.

My husband works hard and he is an astute businessman, and I have to admit that we do well out of it. He sees that I get nice jewelry and things from Damascus, so I don't mind too much that he has to go off on business trips that take him away for two or three weeks. And when he comes back, maybe with some skins of wine from Gaza, we don't have to wait for the next festival before we have a lamb roasted and hire some musicians to play for a dinner party, and I get the chance to dress up. We have a nice house here in Hazor and nice ivories decorating our furniture, from farther away than Damascus—from Assyria and Egypt. We belong to the clan of Naphtali, like everyone around here, and we have some land a little distance from the town, and we employ some servants to look after the land and tend to the animals. They get a share of what they grow there, which isn't a huge amount, but it's enough to live simply on, and they are happy enough given that they had lost their own land because they got into debt.

So, we have a nice house and we are doing okay. And we are grateful to Yahweh for that, and we tithe our income from the business and support the sanctuary here in Hazor. We try to keep the Sabbath, though of course that's hard for a businessman, because if a camel train arrives from Damascus on the Sabbath, he can't just tell them to go away or wait until Sunday.

But those rumors have gotten us worried. Could you tell us exactly what you have been saying about people like us and about a city like ours?

From the prophet Amos in Beth-El
To Makbiram bat Elimelek in Hazor:

> ^{3:13}Listen, and testify against Jacob's household
> (a declaration of the Lord Yahweh, God of
> Armies):
> ¹⁴On the day I attend to Israel's rebellions for it,
> I shall attend to Beth-El's altars. . . .
> ¹⁵I shall strike down the winter house
> as well as the summer house.
> The ivory houses will perish,

the great houses will come to an end
    (Yahweh's declaration). (3:13–15)

4:1Listen to this word,
    you Bashan cows,
You who are on Samaria's mountain,
    you who defraud the poor, who crush the
       needy,
Who say to their husbands,
    'Bring something so we can drink.' . . .
2bThere, days are coming upon you
    when someone will carry you off with
       hooks—
    yes, the last of you with fish hooks.
3Through the breaches you'll go out, each woman
    straight ahead,
    and you'll be thrown out to Harmon
       (Yahweh's declaration). (4:1–3)

6:1Hey, you people who are at peace on Zion,
    who are confident on Samaria's mountain,
You notables of the first of the nations,
    to whom Israel's household come.
2Pass over to Kalneh and look,
    go from there to Great Hamath,
    go down to Gat in Philistia.
Are these better than your kingdoms,
    or their territory than your territory,
3You who push away the bad day,
    but bring near the rule of violence . . . ?
       (6:1–3).

9:1bStrike down the capitals so the thresholds shake;
    break them off on to the head of all of them.

> The last of them I shall kill with the sword;
>> not one of them will flee as a fugitive,
>> no escapee will survive. . . .
> ⁴If they go into captivity before their enemies,
>> from there I shall order the sword and it will
>>> kill them.
> I shall set my eye on them for something bad,
>> not for something good. (9:1b, 4)

Background and Foreground

Makbiram's name appears on a broken jar from an impressive house at Hazor, the huge town north of Lake Galilee, dating from Amos's time. Another broken jar has a name that might be Elimelek or might be Elmattan, so I have given the first name to Ms. Makbiram's father and the second to her husband. Both are names known from the First Testament, though Ms. Makbiram's name doesn't happen to appear there. Also found in the house was a decorated ivory cosmetic spoon and palette which presumably belonged to Ms. Makbiram, an indication that the family was well-to-do. There were other ivory and decorated objects in nearby houses. While prophets like Amos mostly confront the men, who were the people with political power in Israel, occasionally they confront the women, who were no doubt the power behind the throne and certainly profited from their husbands' shady leadership. The introduction to Amos dates his visions during "the two years before the earthquake" (1:1), and Ms. Makbiram's house was one of many places apparently devastated by an earthquake in about 760 BC. Second Kings 15:29 relates how in 732 BC Hazor was attacked and appropriated by the Assyrians, and its people were taken in the first forced migration to Assyria. As usual, what Yahweh did wasn't as bad as he threatened, but it was pretty bad.

A Letter to Amos from the Prophet
Hosea ben Beeri in Samaria

To my lord Amos in Beth-El:

We have never met, but I have heard tell of you, and you have perhaps heard tell of me. I used to go to the festivals at Beth-El, but I have been so appalled at the religious policies of King Jeroboam that I have been boycotting all religious events in recent years.

I think the burden Yahweh has given me is different from the burden he has given you. It's a bit odd in a way, because even though you are working in the sanctuary at Beth-El (I know it's nearer home for you), you are more concerned with corruption in the community, whereas I am working in the capital and I have been more burdened about people's faith, about their misunderstanding of who Yahweh really is and what he wants of them.

But I believe that Yahweh has convinced both of us that disaster is on the way for Ephraim. Yet we also know that Yahweh is the loving God who is committed to Ephraim as his people. And I have a hard time fitting those two facts together. I wonder how you do it. Is it inevitable that Yahweh brings catastrophe to his people? How do we pray in a situation like the one we are in?

From the prophet Amos in Beth-El
To the prophet Hosea ben Beeri in Samaria:

> 7:1The Lord Yahweh showed me this: there, he was forming a locust swarm at the beginning of the growth of the spring crop. There—the spring crop after the king's reaping. 2When it had finished consuming the

grass in the country, I said, 'Lord Yahweh, please pardon, how can Jacob stand, because it's small?' [3]Yahweh relented about this. 'It won't happen,' Yahweh said.

[4]The Lord Yahweh showed me this: there, he was calling for an argument by fire. It consumed the Great Deep and it was consuming the plots.[5] I said, 'Lord Yahweh, please spare, how can Jacob stand, because it's small?' [6]Yahweh relented about this. 'It won't happen either,' the Lord Yahweh said.

[7]He showed me this: there, the Lord was standing by a lead-weight wall, and in his hand was a lead weight. [8]Yahweh said to me, 'What are you looking at, Amos?' I said, 'A lead weight.' The Lord said, 'Here am I, I'm going to put a lead weight in the middle of my people Israel. I shall not again pass over it anymore. [9] Isaac's shrines will be desolate, Israel's sanctuaries will be laid waste. I shall rise against Jeroboam's household with the sword.' . . .

[8:1]The Lord Yahweh showed me this: there, a basket of ripe fruit. [2]He said, 'What are you looking at, Amos?' I said, 'A basket of ripe fruit.' Yahweh said to me, 'The ripe time has come for my people Israel. I shall not again pass over it anymore.' (7:1–9; 8:1–2)

Background and Foreground

There are two sides to a prophet's responsibility. Prophets represent God to people, telling them how God sees things and what God intends (they preach); they also represent people to God, telling God how people see things and what they need (they pray). Amos has a series of visions of things Yahweh might do, which it is his business to share with people. But the visions also push him into prayer; he is clear that one aim of prayer is to get God to relent when he speaks of bringing some catastrophe to people. And he knows that God is fine about his having that aim in prayer.

There is more than one way of reading this sequence of visions and prayers as Amos's reply to Hosea. Twice Amos sees something and prays; then twice he sees things and doesn't pray. Was there once a time when prophets could pray for Yahweh to have mercy and not to bring disaster on Ephraim, but is this time now past? Or is the implication that this time could come, so one cannot assume that such prayer will always be answered, so people had better respond now?

A Letter to Amos from Azaliah ben Hilkiah, Aide to Uzziah, King of Judah

To my lord Amos in Beth-El:

I think you will know that people have been conveying your messages to Jerusalem, though they are not addressed to us, and his majesty King Uzziah has asked me to write to you about them. We know that you are from Tekoa and that you traveled all the way to Beth-El to go and speak in Yahweh's name there. It must have taken you two or three days to get from Tekoa to Beth-El, and we have heard that you stayed here in Jerusalem on the way, but you never stood up in the temple courtyards or came to the palace to say anything here. What we've heard of your preaching in Beth-El makes us feel a bit relieved in a way, but we also feel a bit worried in case there are things we need to hear.

I guess I have three questions. One is whether it's true that you have been saying that Yahweh is going to bring total destruction on Ephraim. You know that relations between Judah and Ephraim have often been tense and sometimes we have fought each other, but it's also the case that we are all part of the same family; we are all descendants of Jacob. So we are concerned for Ephraim.

That question links with the second one. In a way, one can't blame the northern clans for splitting off from Judah and going their own way when they did. His majesty acknowledges that his ancestor King Rehoboam was unwise in the way he refused to moderate the demands that King Solomon had placed on everyone when he was building the temple here (not to say the palace). But the fact remains that the line of David is the one that Yahweh made a commitment to, and eventually the Ephraimites will have to face that fact. And from our point of view, it's grievous that the great Davidic kingdom has been so cut down to size. So I wonder whether you have any word from Yahweh about the future of the Davidic line and the Davidic kingdom.

Which in turn links with a third question. If Yahweh is going to bring catastrophe on Ephraim, are they going to be finished forever? Will there be no future for them? Can Yahweh really cast off most of Ephraim in that way? How would it fit in with his promises? I mean, maybe they would deserve it, but. . . .

From the prophet Amos in Beth-El
To Uzziah King of Judah in Jerusalem:

> 2:4bFor three rebellions by Judah,
>   for four I shall not turn it back,
> Because of their rejecting Yahweh's instruction
>   and not keeping his laws.
> Their lies led them astray,
>   which their ancestors followed.
> 5I shall send off fire against Judah,
>   and it will consume Jerusalem's citadels.
>   (2:4b–5)

⁹:⁸ᶜI shall not totally annihilate
    Jacob's household (Yahweh's declaration).
⁹Because here I am, I'm going to give an order,
    and shake Israel's household among all the
        nations,
As someone shakes in a sieve,
    and no pebble falls to the earth.
¹⁰All the wrongdoers in my people
    will die by the sword,
The people who say, "It won't reach,
    it won't come near us."

¹¹On that day:
    I shall raise David's fallen bivouac,
    and repair its breaches,
I shall raise its ruins,
    and build it up as in days of old,
¹²In order that they may enter into possession of
    what remains of Edom,
    and all the nations that were called by my
        name. . . .

¹³There, days are coming (Yahweh's declaration):
    when the ploughman will reach the reaper,
    the treader of grapes the one trailing the seed.
The mountains will drop sweet wine,
    all the hills will flow.
¹⁴I shall restore the fortunes of my people Israel;
    they'll build up desolate towns and live there.
They'll plant vineyards and drink their wine,
    they will make gardens and eat their fruits.
¹⁵I shall plant them on their land,
    and they won't uproot again
From on their land,

> which I have given them (Yahweh your God
> has said). (9:8–15)

Background and Foreground

No, Yahweh is going to be careful about the way he disciplines Ephraim, Amos says. There aren't as many references to Judah in Amos as there are in Hosea, which is odd, as Amos was a Judahite and Hosea was an Ephraimite. But as there are not many, it draws attention to the two references that do feature. Judah was the last of the seven peoples Amos critiqued in 1:3–2:5. It would have pleased and amused the Ephraimites, until they discovered that they were number eight. But Judah itself needs to note that Yahweh has issued a threat to it. At the other end of the Amos scroll, the threat is balanced by a promise that the reduced nation of Judah will be restored; part of the significance of the reference to Edom will emerge when we come to look at Obadiah. Following on the reference to Judah, the closing promise about Israel looks like a promise about Israel as a whole (Ephraim plus Judah), which makes for a nice finale to the Amos scroll.

A LETTER TO OBADIAH

The best guess about the background of Obadiah is that his prophecy comes from the period after the Babylonians invaded Judah and destroyed Jerusalem, in 587 BC. It's therefore the time when people are praying the prayers in Lamentations, and it's at the end of the time of Jeremiah. Partly by coincidence, this period saw people from Edom drifting northwest and settling in the Negeb, the southern part of Judah. I am imagining Obadiah living in Mizpah, a main center in Judah after the Babylonians made Jerusalem virtually uninhabitable, and the city where Jeremiah lived for a while.

A Letter to Obadiah from Judith bat Jachin of the Clan of Simeon

To my lord Obadiah in Mizpah:

My husband and I are members of the clan of Simeon. I am writing to you on behalf of the two of us, because I am the daughter of a priest and my father taught me to write.

Like the rest of our clan, we lived on land around Beer-Sheba because that area had been the allocation of our clan. Of course, our clan was in an odd situation compared with others, because the area allocated to Simeon was an enclave within the area allocated to Judah, so we were surrounded by Judahites. Relations between us were fine, but Judah was much bigger than us and the Judahites were always much more numerous than us, so we were always under their shadow.

We loved the area around Beer-Sheba, and we loved our life as shepherds with our flocks and our tents. We loved the stark beauty of the wilderness. My husband and his brothers knew where to find a little grass for the sheep and knew even where it was possible to plant some grain and to harvest enough to keep us going. We had a sanctuary at Beer-Sheba; Abraham built an altar there. But some years we were able to go up to Jerusalem for one of the festivals, and it was exciting to be in the big city with its bustle. But we were also glad to get home to the wilderness around Beer-Sheba. We liked to think about Abraham and Sarah and Isaac and Rebecca living there before the actual town of Beer-Sheba existed, and we liked going to the town itself to trade wool for things like pots and tools that we needed.

But that's all past now. Admittedly, we haven't had as hard a time as a result of the Babylonian invasion as people in Jerusalem did. We did have some trouble, when the Babylonian army came this way in order to take on the Egyptians, not long before the fall of Jerusalem. We retreated deeper into the wilderness then, but they found some of us and simply seized our sheep and took our grain. And they caused havoc in Beer-Sheba itself and eventually devastated the town. But it was nothing like what happened to Jerusalem and to the Judahites living around there.

The problem is that it left a kind of power vacuum in the area. Some of our people were already inclined to move north and east, where there was less pressure. And both those developments played into the hands of the Edomites. The Edomites have always been our neighbors to the southeast, down in the Dead Sea Valley and across the other side of the valley. Relations between us have been up and down over the years— sometimes they were our allies, sometimes they were part of our little empire, sometimes they asserted their own independ- ence. They've long been in control of Eilat in the far south, which Judah once controlled. And, as a result of our desire to be independent of Babylon and of the action of the Babylonians that followed, we lost control of much of our area, and the Edomites were able to gain control of it.

The sad thing is that, in a sense, we are all part of the same family. We trace our ancestry back to Jacob and they trace their ancestry back to Esau, and Jacob and Esau were brothers. And we ought to feel sorry for them, because they themselves have been under pressure from the east and south. There are Arab tribes there that have been encroaching on their land. So they've been drifting west and north for years, and the Babylonians have given them the chance to do that in a more concerted way. Remember, the land is wilderness. It doesn't have the fertile areas that you people have to the west. There's hardly enough water for us to look after our sheep and grow our bits of grain. And the Edomites are tough. I don't want to talk about the way Jacob cheated Esau out of his position as Rebecca and Isaac's firstborn son, but I often think about Isaac telling Esau that he would live by the sword. There's a story about our ancestor Simeon wielding a sword once, but he got in trouble with Jacob for it. Since then, we've not been very good with swords.

So when the Edomites started settling in our territory, they pushed us farther north. And with the help of the Babylonians, they didn't just take control of Beer-Sheba. They took control of Hebron. They're not far south of Beth-Lehem now. They're not exactly behaving like members of the family toward us. They took the Babylonians' side when Nebuchadnezzar laid siege to Jerusalem.

So what are we supposed to do? What does Yahweh say about our situation? Is he still committed to us? Is he going to let the Edomites take over the whole country?

From Obadiah in Mizpah
To Judith bat Jachin of the clan of Simeon:

^{1b}The Lord Yahweh has said this about Edom. . . .

> ²Here, I'm making you small among the nations;
>> you're going to be very despised.
> ³The arrogance of your mind has deceived you,
>> you who dwell in the clefts of the crag, the
>>> height of its abode,
> Saying within yourself,
>> 'Who could take me down to earth?'
> ⁴If you go up high like an eagle,
>> if you put your nest among the stars,
>> from there I could bring you down (Yahweh's
>>> declaration). . . .
> ¹⁰Because of the violence to your brother Jacob
>> shame will cover you, and you'll be cut off
>>> permanently.
> ¹¹On the day you stood aside,
>> on the day foreigners captured his resources,
> When aliens came into his gateways,
>> and cast lots for Jerusalem,
>> you, too, were like one of them. . . .

> ^{12b}You shouldn't have rejoiced at the Judahites
>> on the day of their perishing. . . .
> ^{13c}You shouldn't have reached out at his resources
>> on the day of his disaster. . . .

¹⁵Because Yahweh's Day is near against all the
    nations;
  as you did, it will be done to you,
  when your dealings come back on your
    head. . . .

¹⁹The Negeb will possess Mount Esau,
  the Lowland [will possess] the Philistines. . . .
²¹Deliverers will go up on Mount Zion
  to exercise authority over Mount Esau,
  and the kingship will belong to Yahweh.
    (Obadiah 1b–21)

Background and Foreground

In 552 BC the Babylonian king Nabonidus invaded Edom and made it part of his empire, and that empire passed to the Persian king Cyrus in 539 BC. Events over the next couple of centuries are obscure, but late in the Persian period the area became a Persian province and then a Hellenistic province called Idumea. In the 160s BC Judah successfully revolted against Hellenistic rule and reestablished an independent state of Judea; it then made Idumea part of its kingdom, and the Idumeans became Jewish. So you could say that the Edomites didn't get annihilated, but they did eventually get put in their place and converted. Another century later, Judea became part of the Roman Empire, and "Edom" became a cipher for Rome in Jewish thinking. Herod was an Idumean who saw himself as a Jew, and he massively enlarged the Jerusalem temple.

LETTERS TO JONAH

There are several backgrounds to the story of Jonah. First, there is the account of Yahweh giving him a promise that northern Israel would be able to take back land it had lost (see 2 Kings 14:23–27). A second is the position of Assyria as the first great imperial power of Israelite times, a power that could be Yahweh's agent in bringing disaster on Ephraim or Judah but that was also destined to be put down for imposing its authority on other peoples in pursuit of its own interests. A third is the fact that the heyday of Assyria and the heyday of Nineveh when it was Assyria's capital came after Jonah's time, and there are hints that the Hebrew of Jonah comes from later than Jonah's time. So what happened is that Jonah, who was given that promise some time previously, has become the means of telling an imaginative story about the relationship between God's strictness and God's mercy, and about proper attitudes to these characteristics.

A Letter to Jonah from Gershom ben Mahath in Gath-hepher

To my lord Jonah ben Amittay:

Here in Gath-hepher, we are so proud of you! To think that Yahweh would have chosen someone from our little town that no one has heard of to be a prophet to whom he would give a message announcing Yahweh's promise to restore Ephraim to its former glory! To think that we used to look back to the time of Solomon when we controlled all Syria, and then we lost control of it, and then for years the Syrians were harassing us, and here in Gath-hepher we could see their forces coming on raids down the main road from Lake Kinneret that leads to the Mediterranean, and then you said that Yahweh was going to enable us to see them off, and he did! And now you are there on the king's staff in Samaria, able to bring Yahweh's word to him!

But years have passed and situations have changed. Politically speaking, we could get control of Syria only because the Assyrians were looking the other way, and now they're asserting themselves. So our problem isn't the Syrians but the Assyrians, and they are a much more powerful entity, a much more threatening problem. First, we saw their caravans coming down that main road on the way to the Mediterranean and Egypt with their military escorts. And now they've started asserting themselves in the area across the Jordan that you gave your message about. The Assyrians are the ones who control Damascus now. And we hear from merchants that they're engaged in great building projects in their big cities like Nineveh.

Yahweh needs to do something about it. Otherwise, we are soon going to find that they are not merely passing through Ephraim on their way to the Mediterranean. They are going to make us part of their empire. We're going to lose our independence.

So we think that you need to go and consult with Yahweh again about Assyria, the same way as you did about Syria twenty years ago. We need Yahweh to decide to put Assyria in its place the same way as he put Syria in its place. Big empires are no good. Maybe our middle-sized empire that we had under

Solomon wasn't so good either. Maybe Yahweh shouldn't let empires develop. We do have to acknowledge that Solomon developing his empire wasn't such a good idea. It meant he had to make those marriage alliances with Egypt and Moab and Ammon and so on, and to have his wives go and live in Jerusalem and therefore build chapels for them to worship their gods—in Jerusalem!

Whisper it quietly, but we think that King Jeroboam has been pretty problematic in Samaria, as well. They didn't call him Jeroboam for nothing. Jeroboam ben Joash was just like the original Jeroboam, ben Nebat, allegedly serving Yahweh but encouraging a form of spirituality that was too like that of the Canaanites for comfort or for the good of Ephraim. The reason Yahweh enabled us to get our own back on the Syrians wasn't that Ephraim was so committed to Yahweh. It was just that he was merciful to us. It was because he was committed to us despite what we are, not because of who we are. So in a kind of way, it's good that we're back to being something like the size of people that Yahweh's original promise to Abraham spoke of, but not the lords of a great empire. If Yahweh does nothing about the Assyrians, though, they'll end up putting us out of business.

So that's why we think you need to go and consult with Yahweh about Assyria. Maybe he will give you a message about putting them out of business.

From Mibhar ben Joab, scribe, assistant to the Prophet Jonah ben Amittay, now in Jaffa
To Gershom ben Mahath in Gath-hepher:

> 1:1Yahweh's word came to Jonah ben Amittay: 2'Set off, go to the great town of Nineveh and call out against it, because their bad dealing has come up before me.' 3But Jonah set off to flee to Tarshish from before Yahweh.

He went down to Jaffa, found a ship going to Tarshish, paid its fare, and went down into it to go with them to Tarshish from before Yahweh. ⁴But Yahweh flung a great wind into the sea, there was a great storm in the sea, and the ship threatened to break up. ⁵The sailors were afraid and cried out each of them to his god. They flung the things that were in the ship into the sea to lighten it of them.

Jonah had gone down into the inmost parts of the vessel, lain down, and gone to sleep. ⁶The captain went to see him and said to him: 'What are you doing, sleeping? Get up, call on your god. Perhaps the god will give a thought to us and we won't perish.'

⁷The men said to each other, 'Come on, let's make lots fall so we can know on whose account this bad fate has come to us.' They made lots fall, and the lot fell on Jonah. ⁸They said to him, 'Tell us, please, on whose account this bad fate has come to us. What's your work? Where do you come from? What's your country? What people are you from?' ⁹He said to them, 'I'm a Hebrew. I live in awe of Yahweh the God of the heavens, who made the sea and the dry land.'

¹⁰The men were greatly afraid and said to him, 'What is this you've done?,' when the men knew that he was fleeing from before Yahweh, when he had told them. ¹¹They said to him, 'What shall we do to you so that the sea quietens down from upon us?' (when the sea was growing stormier). ¹²He said to them, 'Lift me up and hurl me into the sea, and the sea will quieten down from upon you, because I acknowledge that it was on my account that this great storm has come upon you.'

¹³The men rowed to get back to dry land, but they couldn't, because the sea was growing stormier against

them. ¹⁴They called to Yahweh, 'Oh, Yahweh, may we please not perish for this man's life. Don't put upon us the blood of someone free of guilt. Because you, Yahweh—as you wished, you have acted.' ¹⁵They lifted Jonah up and hurled him into the sea; and the sea stopped its raging. ¹⁶The men were in great awe of Yahweh. They offered a sacrifice to Yahweh and made pledges.

¹⁷Yahweh provided a big fish to swallow Jonah, and Jonah was in the fish's insides three days and three nights. (1:1–17)

Background and Foreground

Jonah and his assistant (like the average Israelite) give no indication of being against foreigners, and the story portrays foreigners such as Jonah's sailors as neither wicked nor stupid. Actually, they seem to have been wiser than Jonah. But Jonah (representing other Israelites, we may guess) does want to see Yahweh act against the Assyrians, because they are an imperial power that as such wants to get economic control of their world and make it run in a way they can profit from more than anyone else. And Yahweh is committed to putting down such imperial powers.

But why, exactly, does Yahweh want Jonah to go and preach against them? Why not just annihilate them? In cowboy films and gangster films, killers often want to tell their victims why they're killing them (and often they then get into trouble through delaying their action). Maybe it's partly that they feel the need to justify their action to themselves, and they want their victims to know that their death takes place in a moral universe and the scriptwriters want to affirm that, too. And maybe there is something similar about Yahweh's action. But it will become clear that there is more to it than this. And why, further, does Jonah not want to go and do as Yahweh says? This, too, will become clearer in due course.

A Letter to Jonah from his Assistant
Mibhar ben Joab in Jaffa

To my lord Jonah ben Amittay:

What I want to know is not what kind of fish it was. Presumably it's impossible in the normal course of events for a man to be swallowed by a fish and to stay alive, and therefore it's interesting to wonder about that question, but I know that Yahweh can do the impossible, and it's not the important question. What I want to know is, how did you pray when you were swallowed by the fish? I can think of two sorts of thing that I would want to say to God in the circumstances. I've heard it said that two of the best prayers anyone ever prays are, "Help, help, help," and "Sorry, sorry, sorry." Your story reminds me of that! What I imagine I would be doing is confessing the wrong I had done in sailing off in the opposite direction from the one that God said, and assuring God that I had learned my lesson and that I would do as he ordered next time. And I would be pleading with him to get the fish to spew me out so I could get back onto the shore. I assume you were not far from dry land, because ships don't simply sail straight across the Mediterranean, they hug the coastline. So you wouldn't be far from the shore.

From the prophet Jonah ben Amittay, now in Nineveh
To Mibhar ben Joab, back in Jaffa:

> 2:2Out of my pressure I called
> to Yahweh and he answered me.
> When I called for help from Sheol's belly,
> you listened to my voice.
> 3You threw me into the deep,
> into the heart of the seas.

The river surrounded me;
  all your breakers and your waves passed
    over me.
⁴I myself said, 'I've been driven away
  from in front of your eyes.'
Yet I shall again look
  towards your sacred palace.
⁵The water overwhelmed me, up to my neck,
  the deep surrounded me.
Reed was wrapped around my head
  ⁶at the roots of the mountains.
I went down into the earth,
  its bars were about me permanently.
But you got my life up from the Pit,
  Yahweh my God.
⁷When my life was ebbing away from me,
  I was mindful of Yahweh.
My plea came to you,
  to your sacred palace.
⁸People who keep watch for things that are empty
    and hollow
  forsake their commitment.
⁹But I—with a voice of thanksgiving I will
    sacrifice to you;
  for what I have pledged I shall make good—
  deliverance belongs to Yahweh. (2:2–9)

Background and Foreground

How wrong Mibhar ben Joab was! Jonah does no confessing here. What we will read later fits with that, even though Jonah has admitted that he was responsible for the imperiling of the ship, not to say the loss of its cargo. Nor does he do any asking. What he says to Yahweh is dominated by what has been called another of the great prayers, "Thank you, thank you, thank you." So either we are to imagine this act of praise is one that he undertakes inside the fish in anticipation of the moment when the fish will have spewed him out, or it is the act of praise that he undertakes inside the fish because the fish is the means of his deliverance; it meant he didn't drown. Either way, in effect Jonah has been in Sheol's belly, he has been in the Pit, he has been as good as dead. But he knew he could and must look to Yahweh's palace in the heavens (which he could do even inside the fish!) and that Yahweh had responded to him there.

A Follow-Up to Jonah from Gershom ben Mahath in Gath-hepher

To my lord Jonah ben Amittay in Nineveh:

In light of your assistant's account of what happened to you, I am thoroughly confused. If Yahweh told you to go to Nineveh to inveigh against it, why did you go in the opposite direction? It sounds as if it would be just the commission we wanted Yahweh to give you. Actually, we would have expected to see you coming via Gath-hepher on your way to Nineveh! We could have had a great celebration of what Yahweh was going to do in putting the Assyrians down! No wonder Yahweh chased you when you sailed off in the opposite direction! Those poor foreign sailors! So what are you going to do now? We think you should check with Yahweh again. Maybe he will exonerate you for sailing off across the Mediterranean and re-commission you. Maybe we'll still get the chance of that celebration and see the smoke rising from Nineveh.

From Mibhar ben Joab, scribe, assistant to the prophet Jonah
ben Amittay in Nineveh
To Gershom ben Mahath in Gath-hepher:

3:1Yahweh's word came to Jonah a second time: 2'Set
off, go to the great town of Nineveh and call out to it
the thing that I'm going to speak to you.' 3Jonah set
off and went to Nineveh in accordance with Yahweh's
word. Now Nineveh was an extraordinarily great town,
three days walk through. 4Jonah started to go through
the town, one day's walk. He called out, 'Forty days
more, and Nineveh will be overthrown.' 5The Ninevites
believed God and called for a fast and put on sack,
from the biggest of them to the least of them.

6The word reached the king of Nineveh, and he
got up from his throne, took off his robe from upon
him, covered himself with sack, and sat on ash. 7He got
people to cry out in Nineveh, by the decree of the king
and his big people: 'Human being and animal (cattle
and flock) are not to taste anything. They're not to
pasture; they're not to drink water. 8They're to cover
themselves in sack, human being and animal, and call
on God strongly. They're to turn, each one from his bad
way and from the violence that's in their fists. 9Who
knows, God may turn back and relent, turn back from
his anger, and we may not perish.'

10God saw their actions, that they turned back from
their bad way, and God relented of the bad thing that
he had spoken about doing to them. He didn't do it.

4:1But it seemed bad to Jonah, a very bad thing. He
was enraged.

2He prayed to Yahweh: 'Oh, Yahweh, isn't this what
I said when I was in my country? That's why I acted

previously by fleeing to Tarshish, because I knew that you're a God gracious, compassionate, long-tempered, vast in commitment, and relenting about something bad. [3]So now, Yahweh, please take my life from me, because my dying will be good, better than my living.'

[4]Yahweh said, 'Was your rage good?'

[5]Jonah went out from the town and sat east of the town. He made a bivouac for himself there and sat under it in the shade until he could see what would happen in the town. [6]Yahweh God provided a qiqayon vine and it grew up over Jonah so as to be a shade over his head to rescue him from what was bad for him. Jonah rejoiced greatly about the qiqayon. [7]But God provided a worm when dawn came up next day and it struck down the qiqayon, and it withered; [8]and when the sun rose, God provided a scorching east wind, and the sun struck down on Jonah's head. He grew faint and asked for his life, that he might die. He said, 'My dying will be good, better than my living.'

[9]God said to Jonah, 'Was your rage good about the qiqayon?' He said, 'It was good, my rage, to the point of death.' [10]Yahweh said, 'You pitied the qiqayon, for which you didn't labour and which you didn't grow, which came into existence overnight and perished overnight. [11]Shouldn't I pity the great town of Nineveh, in which there are more than 120,000 human beings who don't know their right hand from their left, and many animals?' (3:1–4:11)

Background and Foreground

The second half of the story explains that Jonah has understood more than one might have thought. He knew that Yahweh is committed to putting down oppressive powers, but he also knew that Yahweh is even keener on the idea of them turning from their wrongdoing. Joel has referred to these facts about Yahweh that Jonah speaks of (Joel 2:12–14), and Jonah would be glad that they apply to Israel. He's not so keen on imperial oppressors turning and escaping. He thinks oppressors should be punished. Yet most of the one hundred and twenty thousand "who don't know their right hand from their left" (Jonah 4:11) wouldn't be directly involved in the formulating of imperial policy, though they likely would be beneficiaries of it. As Yahweh doesn't give up on Nineveh, however, neither does he give up on Jonah. He tries to get through to him by means of the qiqayon vine (we don't know what that was) and the worm and the hot wind. We don't discover if he succeeded. Mibhar ben Joab leaves Gershom ben Mahath to think about Yahweh's question for himself.

LETTERS TO
MICAH

Micah was a contemporary of Amos and of Isaiah. He
came from a town that was down the mountain slopes
west of Jerusalem, a couple of days' walk away from the capital. He's like Amos in being a master communicator, not
least in getting people's attention and then kicking them
in the teeth. So he starts off by talking about the sins of
Samaria, and one can imagine people nodding with approval
in Jerusalem; then he turns to the sins of Jerusalem itself. He
starts from the fact that his home lies in the region that has
first experience of any invasion of Judah that happens—it's
the direction from which invading armies often come—and
he exploits that fact. The Jerusalemites have heard of Gath
and Shaphir and Beth-Leaphrah and Lachish and Adullam
and so on. He encourages them to think about the names of
these places (Micah 1:2–16)—the first letter refers back to
this. His actual message compares with Isaiah's in declaring that Judah is in trouble because of what is wrong in its
attitude to Yahweh and in people's relationships with one
another, that trouble is therefore coming, but that this is not
the end of the story.

A Letter to Micah from Asiel ben Mibsam, President of the Elders in Lachish

To my lord Micah of Moresheth in Jerusalem:

My colleagues and I are concerned about the way your preaching is endangering morale here in Lachish. Our city is not the capital of Judah and we do not have the temple here, nor does the king have a palace here. Yet there is a case for saying that Lachish is at least as important as Jerusalem in its own way. Or at least there is a case for saying that our city is vitally important to Jerusalem. We guard the western approaches to Jerusalem. As someone who lived not far from here yourself, you know that we are way more important than any other Judahite city outside Jerusalem. The most practical route for an army to get to Jerusalem involves coming this way.

We have to admit that you were clever the way you lulled us into a false sense of security with your preaching. You summoned the nations of the world to court and gave the impression that you were about to condemn them for their wrongdoing. Then you remonstrated about the wrongdoing of Samaria, which is always a good way to get people cheering in Judah. Then you turned on Jerusalem itself, and that can also go down well out here in the foothills. But the trouble is that you eventually turned on us.

We also have to admit that you were then clever in the way you played with our names. You bade people not to tell Gath about an invasion; and Gath was the town David bade people not to tell about the death of Saul and Jonathan! Saying to people in Beth-Leaphrah, whose name sounds as if it is a house of dirt, that they should roll in the dirt! Telling the people in Shaphir, "Beautiful," that they are going to end up naked and shamed! And telling us to get our "chariots" ready, which over-laps with our name, and then implying we would be getting them ready so we can run away! We hereby say to you: Lachish is not a city whose people run away! We have solid walls and we can withstand any siege. Yet you turned our strength into a sin, as if having that military strength and those battle resources was somehow wrong!

From Micah of Moresheth
To Asiel ben Mibsam:

> 2:1Hey, you people thinking up trouble,
>   doing something bad on their beds.
> At morning light they do it,
>   because it's in the power of their hand.
> 2They desire fields and steal them—
>   houses, and take them.
> They defraud a man and his household,
>   an individual and his domain.

> 3Therefore Yahweh has said this:

> Here am I, thinking up a bad fate for this kin-group
>   that you won't move your neck away from.
> You won't walk tall,
>   because it will be a bad time.

> 4On that day,
>   someone will lift up a poem against you,
>   he'll wail with a wail, a wailing.
> He's saying, 'We are destroyed, destroyed,
>   he exchanges my people's share.
> Aagh, he removes it from me,

he shares out our fields to someone who
    turns away.'
⁵Therefore there will be no one for you
    casting the cord by lot
    in Yahweh's congregation.

⁶'Don't preach,' they preach,
    'people are not to preach about these things.
Disgrace won't turn away
    ⁷ᵃ(should it be said, Jacob's household?).
Has Yahweh's temper become short,
    are these things his acts?' . . .

¹⁰Set off, go,
    because this won't be a place to settle,
On account of defilement that will destroy
    with a grave destruction.
¹¹If someone were going about
    with wind and deceptive falsehood,
'I shall preach to you about wine and about
        liquor,'
    he'd be this people's preacher. (2:1–7a, 10–11)

Background and Foreground

The bulk of the elders' letter takes up that message in Micah 1, which was mostly a warning about Yahweh bringing trouble to Judah but said little about the reasons for it. This second message begins with a critique that articulates the reasons. As is the case when Amos talks about life in Ephraim, the critique focuses on the way people who are doing well are able to take over the land of people who are in economic trouble. The punishment will fit the crime. The takeover experts are destined to lose their own land when the invasion happens. They also will lose the right to take part in the meetings that decide on allocations of land. Meanwhile, people who are their victims might as well get out of here, given the destruction that is coming. Micah also comments on the way the people with power are trying to stop him preaching and makes an acerbic comment about the kind of preacher who would suit them.

A Letter to Micah from the Prophet Maon ben Gazez

To my lord Micah of Moresheth in Jerusalem:

I'm writing on behalf of the prophets of Judah in support of the message from the Lachish elders. Our vocation as prophets is to bring people a message from the God of Israel, the God of love and grace and mercy. You talk about him as if he were a God of wrath, as if he were always threatening to discipline us, to bring catastrophe. But all through our history Yahweh has been proving himself to us as a God who promises well-being to his people. He speaks of *shalom*. His plans for his people involve well-being, not trouble, to give them a future with hope. It's our privilege to live by trust in him, to lean on him. He is in our midst.

In our time, people especially need a hopeful message, not a negative one. Every year the threat of Assyrian rule becomes more real. Every year the possibility of Assyrian invasion becomes more plausible, especially for those of us who live in the foothills between Jerusalem and the Mediterranean and who are therefore on an army's route into the highland. In light of these threats, every year the way the authorities in Jerusalem formulate policy becomes more problematic. People need our support, not our attack. We agree with the elders. In Yahweh's name, you must stop.

From Micah of Moresheth
To Maon ben Gazez:

> ³:¹I said, 'Listen, please, heads of Jacob,
>   rulers of Israel's household:
> It's for you to know how to exercise authority,
>   isn't it,
>   ²people who are hostile to what is good and
>   loyal to what is bad,
> Who tear the skin from on my people,
>   their flesh from on their bones,
> ³Who eat my people's flesh
>   and strip off their skin from on them,
> Break up their bones,
>   cut them up as in a pan,
>   like meat inside a pot.'
> ⁴Then they will cry out to Yahweh,
>   but he will not answer them.
> He will hide his face from them at that time,
>   as they've acted badly in their practices.

> ⁵Yahweh has said this:

> About the prophets who lead my people astray,
>   who chew with their teeth and call out that
>   things will be well,
> But someone who puts nothing in their mouths—
>   they declare a sacred battle against him.
> ⁶Therefore there will be night for you, without
>   vision,
>   darkness for you, without divination.
> The sun will set for the prophets,
>   the day will be dark for them.

7The seers will be ashamed,
  the diviners confounded.
All of them will cover over their lip,
  because there's no answer from God.
8But as for me, I'm full of energy, with
      Yahweh's wind,
    and strong authority,
To tell Jacob about its rebellion,
  Israel about its wrongdoing.

9Listen to this, please,
  heads of Jacob's household,
  rulers of Israel's household,
You who take offence at the exercise of authority,
  and make what is straight crooked,
10One who builds Zion with bloodshed,
  Jerusalem with evil.
11Its heads exercise authority for a bribe,
  its priests teach for a fee.
Its prophets divine for money,
  but lean on Yahweh:
'Yahweh is among us, isn't he,
  bad fortune won't come upon us.'
12Therefore, on account of you,
  Zion will be a field that is ploughed.
Jerusalem will become ruins,
  the house's mount a great shrine in a forest.
        (3:1–12)

Background and Foreground

If there were prophets who literally referred to Yahweh promising well-being to his people, speaking of *shalom*, having plans that involve well-being, not trouble, and that give them a future with hope, then they were anticipating Jeremiah (see Jeremiah 29:11). And there is actually a direct link between Micah and Jeremiah. When Jeremiah said Jerusalem was going to be destroyed, the prophets of his day said that he should be put to death. But the elders of his day reminded people that Micah had spoken about Zion becoming a plowed field and that Micah had not been put to death. In fact, they said, it drove King Hezekiah to pray, and God relented (see Jeremiah 26).

Already in Micah's context, promising well-being, promising *shalom*, is a fair summary of the message that prophets gave. They are the people one might call the false prophets, but the First Testament just calls them the prophets, with an implication that they are the "regular" prophets. Someone like Micah who brings a tough message is the odd one out. Like the priests, the other prophets get paid for their work as ministers, but being paid skews their ministry. No doubt most prophets did sincerely believe that they had a vocation to be encouraging to the community in a context when it needed encouragement.

Micah sees that there is a link between the threat that everyone sees hanging over Judah and the way the people with power in Judah are behaving towards ordinary people. They have power in government or business or education or worship, and they can make sure that they themselves are doing okay, even if things are hard for ordinary people. Ultimately, if not directly, they take away people's lives by the way they make the financial and economic system work. But Micah has power, too, the kind of power that belongs to the wind when Yahweh makes the wind blow.

Did the other prophets say he was just a windy prophet, as the Ephraimites said about Hosea? But he has strength and authority the same as the people in power have, because he brings Yahweh's message.

A Letter to Micah from the Prophet Isaiah ben Amoz

To my lord Micah of Moresheth:

It is of course a great encouragement to me that you proclaim to the people of Judah the same sort of message as I do! I am especially struck by the way we both affirm that Yahweh is not finished either with Zion or with David. He made a commitment to both of them way back, and he will surely keep that commitment in the long run. In other words, while the prophets who promise well-being do not speak the truth now, they make promises that will ultimately come true.

I like the way your promise about Zion is set against both what you said earlier about Zion itself and what you said about the nations. You began by urging the nations to listen and by half-implying that Yahweh is giving testimony against them. But if he was doing that, it was not his last word for them, either. Because Yahweh is going to draw them to Zion to learn about Yahweh's ways and to listen to his teaching. If only Judah and Ephraim were so inclined! It would mean that the kind of conflict we hear about between Syria on one hand and Ammon and Moab and Edom on the other will be a thing of the past, because Yahweh will have sorted things out for them. You've also properly lambasted Zion itself for being built on bloodshed: what a terrible expression! So if Zion is to be set on high and to draw the nations to it in a positive way, it must mean Zion is different. I wonder what you think is Yahweh's implied challenge to Zion now?

You are more subtle in your critique of Ahaz and Hezekiah than I am! And when you talk about a king and about someone who reigns, you are more often referring to Yahweh than to Ahaz or Hezekiah. You haven't abandoned Yahweh's promise to David, but with some subtlety you don't mention him—you only refer to Beth-Lehem and thus to someone whose origin lies long ago. So you suggest that Yahweh will do something that is new but old, something in continuity with the old but in discontinuity with the kingship that we experience. Like the original king from Beth-Lehem, he'll be a shepherd, which implies authority but also implies providing and not plundering. But who is his mother? You describe her as one who is going to give birth, which is the same expression as I used in my message to Ahaz about a girl who is going to have a baby! He too will be a "ruler" rather than a king. And will he care about the northern Israelites as well as the Judahites, or are they finished?

From Micah of Moresheth
To Isaiah ben Amoz:

> 4:1 At the end of the time
>> the mountain of Yahweh's house will be
> Established at the head of the mountains,
>> elevated above the hills.
> Peoples will stream to it;
>> 2many nations will go and say,
> 'Come, let's go up to Yahweh's mountain,
>> to the house of Jacob's God,
> So he may teach us in his ways
>> and we may walk in his paths.'
> Because instruction will go out from Zion,
>> Yahweh's word from Jerusalem.
> 3He will decide between many peoples
>> and issue reproof for numerous nations, even
>>> far away.
> They'll beat their swords into hoes,
>> their spears into pruning hooks.
> Nation won't take up sword against nation;
>> they will no more learn about battle.

⁴They will sit, each person,
    under his vine and under his fig tree,
With no one disturbing—
    because the mouth of Yahweh of Armies has
        spoken.
⁵Because all the peoples walk,
    each in the name of its god,
But we ourselves will walk
    in the name of Yahweh our God lastingly and
        permanently.

⁶On that day (Yahweh's declaration):

I shall gather the lame, collect the ones driven out,
    and those to whom I've done something bad.
⁷I shall turn the lame into a remainder,
    the outcast into a numerous nation.
Yahweh will reign over them on Mount Zion,
    from now and permanently. . . .

⁹Now, why do you issue a shout,
    is there not a king in you?
Has your counselor perished,
    that writhing has taken strong hold of you like
        a woman giving birth? . . .
¹⁰ᶜYou will come as far as Babylon,
    but there you will be rescued.
There Yahweh will restore you
    from the fist of your enemies. (4:1–10)

⁵:²But you, Beth-Lehem in Ephratah,
    small to be among Judah's clans,
From you will emerge for me
    someone to be a ruler in Israel,

whose emerging is of old, of ancient days.
³Therefore he will give them up until the time
  when the one who is going to give birth has
    given birth,
And those who are left of his brothers
  come back to the Israelites.
⁴ᵃHe will stand and shepherd with Yahweh's vigour,
  in the majesty of the name of Yahweh his
    God. (5:2–4a)

Background and Foreground

The answer to Isaiah's final question lies in Micah 5:3. The one who is going to give birth might be Ms. Zion or might be Ms. Beth-Lehem or might be Ms. Judah, but one can't blame Christian readers for finding Mary here. The answer to Isaiah's earlier question about Micah's challenge to Zion now lies in 4:5, which issues a challenge to Judah in their day. That question draws attention to another one that is intriguing but unanswerable. Isaiah 2:2–4 itself includes the same promise about Yahweh's house that Micah 4:1–3 gives. Perhaps Yahweh made this promise through Micah (and the Isaiah scroll also includes it), or perhaps he made it through Isaiah (and the Micah scroll also includes it), or perhaps he made it through someone else (and they both include it from there). The fact that it comes twice in the Prophets may hint that it is important!

A Letter to Micah from King Hezekiah ben Ahaz

To my lord Micah of Moresheth:

There's a line of yours that I wonder about. Here's one version of it:

He has told you, people, what is good,
   what Yahweh requires from you:
Only justice, and loving faithfulness,
   and walking humbly with your God.

The trouble is, people make it mean lots of different things. Can you explain it? The words are vague, really. What do you mean by justice? It's a rather abstract word, and it means so many different things to different people. Loving is the same: when I tell my little son I love him, it's mostly a feeling. And faithfulness: how long does one carry on being faithful when people aren't faithful? The questions are practical ones for me. As king, I have some responsibility for justice. The very word suggests exercising authority, making executive decisions. What sort of things should I focus on? I know that loving isn't actually just a feeling; it's an action. So how do I love Yahweh by my actions? We express our love in our worship. We make sacrifices. How big do the sacrifices need to be to show Yahweh that we mean our love? I have responsibility for faithfulness, for seeing that people keep their commitments to Yahweh and to one another. How do I do that? I have to face the fact that we may well be under military threat, because the Assyrians have an insatiable appetite for expanding their empire. Faced with that fact, what does walking humbly with Yahweh mean? Does it mean trusting him to look after us and not taking any action to provide ourselves with defense?

From Micah of Moresheth
To King Hezekiah ben Ahaz:

> 5:9Your hand will rise over your adversaries,
>   and all your enemies will be cut off.

10On that day (Yahweh's declaration):

I shall cut down your horses from among you,
    and obliterate your chariots.
[11]I shall cut down the towns in your country,
    and tear down all your fortresses.
[12]I shall cut down the charms from your hand,
    and you will have no chanters.
[13]I shall cut down your images
    and your pillars from among you.
You will not bow low any more
    to something made by your hands.
[14]I shall uproot your totem poles from among you
    and annihilate your towns. (5:9–14)

6:10Shall I forget the faithless household,
    the faithless storehouses,
    the condemned short measure?
[11]Would I be clean with faithless scales,
    with a bag of false weights?—
[12]Whose rich people are full of violence,
    whose inhabitants speak falsehood,
    and their tongue is deceit in their mouths? . . .

[15]You—you'll sow but not harvest;
    you—you'll tread olives but not rub with oil,
    and grapes but not drink wine.
16aYou've kept Omri's laws,
    every practice of Ahab's household. (6:10–16a)

6:6By what means shall I meet Yahweh,
    bow down to God on High?
Shall I meet him by means of burnt offerings,
    bullocks a year old?
[7]Would Yahweh accept thousands of rams,
    in myriads of streams of oil?

Should I give my firstborn for my rebellion,
    the fruit of my body for my own wrongdoing?
8aHe has told you, people, what is good. (6:6–8a)

Background and Foreground

These messages from Micah that I imagine addressed to King
Hezekiah start with a promise that Judah will win a great victory
over the Assyrians. They will be "cut off" (5:9). But that promise
leads into a declaration that Yahweh threatens to "cut down"
Judah's military resources and its religious resources. Putting the
promise and the threat next to each other implies that people can
have the victory only if they take note of the warnings.

The next paragraph's description of corruption denotes
practices that correspond to the laws and practices of Omri and
Ahab, who ruled in Ephraim a century previously (see 1 Kings
21:1–14). So it's quite an insult. The account of Ahab also makes
a specific reference to someone offering his sons as a human
sacrifice, with an implication that Ahab at least tolerated it (see
1 Kings 16:34). So the question about what kind of sacrifice one
might make to Yahweh is not just a theoretical one. In effect,
Hezekiah's letter shows that he knew what Yahweh actually
regarded as "good." First, it means seeing that power is exercised
in a way that expresses faithfulness and encourages faithfulness.
Then it means deferring to Yahweh rather than trusting that you
know what to do and relying on your resources.

A Letter to Micah from Azariah ben Uriah, Priest in Jerusalem

To my lord Micah of Moresheth:

I have several questions to put to you, but really they are all
aspects of one question. Do you think you are being more bleak

about Judah than is justified? There might be two senses in which you are being over-gloomy. One is that your assessment of the people is so negative. I am engaged in a ministry at the temple, and people don't seem so bad. Some of them show up at daybreak and at dusk when we offer the morning and evening sacrifices. Families come to bring offerings when a mother has given birth safely and the baby is okay. Is it the case that I see them at their best, and the way they are when they go home is quite different?

Even if you're right in your assessment of the people, I also wonder whether you are too gloomy in threatening that Yahweh is really going to be so severe in disciplining us. And if you are right, what I'm not clear about is how that threat relates to the description Yahweh gave us of himself at Sinai. Yahweh did bring terrible chastisement upon us there, and it might have been the end, and in fact Yahweh told Moses it would be the end, but Moses persuaded him to change his mind. In that connection, he gave Moses that profound description of himself as a God who is compassionate and gracious, long-tempered, big in commitment and truthfulness, guarding commitment to thousands, carrying waywardness and rebellion and wrongdoing. Is it still true?

From Micah of Moresheth
To Azariah ben Uriah, Priest in Jerusalem:

> 7:1a Aagh, me, because I've become
>> like the gatherings of summer fruit,
>> like the gleanings of the vintage. . . .
> 2 The committed person has perished from the
>> country,
>> there's no one upright among the people. . . .
> 5 Don't believe a neighbour,
>> don't rely on a friend.

From the one who sleeps in your embrace
     guard the opening of your mouth.
6Because son acts villainously to father,
     daughter rises up against her mother,
Daughter-in-law against her mother-in-law;
     a person's enemies are the people in his
          household.
7But I myself will look to Yahweh,
     I shall wait for my God who delivers me;
     my God will listen to me.

8Don't rejoice over me, my enemy;
     when I've fallen, I'm getting up.
When I sit in darkness,
     Yahweh will be my light.
9I shall carry Yahweh's wrath
     when I've done wrong to him,
Until he gives judgment for me
     and exercises authority for me.
He will get me out into the light,
     I shall see his faithfulness. . . .

17bMay they come trembling out of their strongholds
     to Yahweh our God,
     may they be in dread and awe of you.
18Who is a God like you, one who carries
          waywardness,
     and passes over rebellion for the remainder of
          his domain.
He doesn't keep strong hold of his anger
          permanently,
     because he delights in commitment;
19When he has compassion on us again, he'll
     trample on our wayward acts;

> he'll throw all our wrongdoings into the
> depths of the sea.
> [20]You will show truthfulness to Jacob,
> commitment to Abraham,
> as you swore to our ancestors from days
> of old. (7:1a, 2–9, 17–20)

Background and Foreground

It looks as if Micah would think the priest is more positive about the people than is justified. There can be a clash between what people are like when they go to worship and what they are like at home and at work. Indeed, Micah's account of life in Jerusalem makes it sound like an excerpt from a spy story.

On the other hand, he wouldn't think the priest is overly positive in the way he looks at Yahweh. Indeed, Micah adds a pair of vivid images of his own to a confirmation of Yahweh's words at Sinai. Yahweh will trample on our wayward acts like an army trampling on its foes; he will throw our wrongdoings into the depths of the sea from where they cannot be retrieved.

LETTERS TO NAHUM

The Nahum scroll begins by telling the readers that it is a pronouncement about Nineveh, which was the capital of the Assyrian Empire in the seventh century. So we are now a century after Micah's day. Nahum doesn't talk about Jerusalem or Zion, and he makes only one mention of Judah, in promising that it will become free when Yahweh brings about the destruction of Nineveh. The destruction and thus the fall of the Assyrian Empire happened as Nahum promised in 612 BC at the hands of the Babylonians and Medes. The event would have vindicated Nahum, which is presumably one factor in establishing that he was a true prophet of Yahweh and in leading to his scroll finding a place among the Scriptures.

A Letter to Nahum from Hilkiah ben Shallum, Priest in Jerusalem

To my lord Nahum of Elkosh:

My revered ancestor Azariah asked the prophet Micah of Moresheth whether we could still take for granted Yahweh's great description of himself as compassionate and gracious, long-tempered, big in commitment and truthfulness, guarding commitment to thousands, carrying waywardness and rebellion and wrongdoing. It was a gloomy question, though he blamed Micah for his gloom, and Micah gave him a reassuring answer.

I have another reason for thinking about that description of Yahweh. There's a story about an earlier prophet, Jonah of Amittay, going to Nineveh to proclaim Yahweh's message to it. He told the Ninevites that their city was going to be conquered, and they turned from their wrongdoing and their violence. Yahweh therefore relented of his plan for their city to be conquered. Jonah was not pleased, because he was looking forward to them getting their just reward, and Yahweh reminded him of that description of himself that Micah confirmed. Actually, Jonah knew already that it wasn't just a description of Yahweh's stance in relation to Judah. It could apply to an oppressive imperial power like the Assyrians. That's why he didn't want to encourage them to change and escape judgment.

I confess I have a lot of sympathy for Jonah. If the Assyrians actually had turned from their wrongdoing and violence, then I hope I would be glad for Yahweh to turn away from the intention to overthrow them. It would be great if Assyria could become a benevolent, generous, fair-minded empire! What an excellent idea! But empires don't become empires or stay empires by being benevolent, generous, and fair-minded. We in Judah are not the only people in a position to testify to that. Ask anyone around. Ask the Philistines. King Sargon of Assyria boasted about the way he had taken them in Micah's day, in between giving the same treatment to all Judah except for Jerusalem itself.

When Yahweh described himself to Moses as compassionate and gracious, long-tempered, big in commitment and truthfulness, guarding commitment to thousands, carrying waywardness and rebellion and wrongdoing, he went on to add that he didn't just acquit people. He attended to the waywardness of people in a way that also affected the following generations.

So how does all this apply to Nineveh in our day?

From Nahum of Elkosh
To Hilkiah ben Shallum, Priest in Jerusalem:

> [1:2]Yahweh is a God who is passionate and takes redress;
> Yahweh takes redress and is a possessor of
> wrath.
> Yahweh takes redress on his adversaries,
> maintains it towards his enemies.
> [3]Yahweh is long-tempered but big in energy,
> and certainly doesn't treat people as free of
> guilt.
> Yahweh—his way is in whirlwind and in storm,
> the cloud is the dust from his feet.
> [4]He reprimands the sea and withers it,
> dries up all the rivers.
> Bashan and Carmel languish,
> Lebanon's blossom languishes.
> [5]Mountains quake because of him,
> the hills melt.
> The earth lifts from before him,
> the world and all the people who live in it.
> [6]Before his condemnation, who can stand,
> and who can rise against his angry burning?—
> His wrath pours out like fire,
> and crags shatter because of him.
> [7]Yahweh is good, a stronghold on the day of
> pressure,
> and he acknowledges people who take shelter
> with him. (1:2–7)

> [2:6]The river gates open, the palace melts;
> [7]it's decreed: it's exiled, it's taken up.
> Its handmaids lament like the voice of doves,
> beating on their chests.

⁸Nineveh was like a pool of water of old,
    but they're fleeing.
'Stop, stop,'
    but no one can turn them. (2:6–8)

Background and Foreground

There is a wicked cleverness about the way Nahum starts
with his description of Yahweh. In its form (adjectives and par-
ticiples), it's just like that self-description that Yahweh gave
at Sinai. But in its content, it's the exact opposite—though in
the same context at Sinai Yahweh does also describe himself
as passionate, and elsewhere the Torah speaks of his taking
redress and expressing wrath. Again, at Sinai Yahweh described
himself as long-tempered—but that doesn't mean never finally
saying, "That's it." Furthermore, he affirmed there that he
certainly doesn't acquit people as if they have integrity when
they don't, and Nahum here repeats the same expression. So
Yahweh lives with the tension between being the God of love
and the God who cannot simply turn a blind eye to evil, and he
has to decide from time to time when and how to give expression to the first or to the second. And for Nineveh, this is a
moment when it's time to treat a guilty city as guilty. Judah
will not be doing the destroying, but Yahweh's action will also
mean relief for Judah.

A Follow-Up to Nahum from Hilkiah
ben Shallum, Priest in Jerusalem

To my lord Nahum of Elkosh:

My colleagues and I have been discussing the implications
of your message that Yahweh is going to overturn Nineveh, as
Jonah once said. Different ones of us raised different questions.

First, is Yahweh fair? Micah declared that Jerusalem itself would be overturned, and it hasn't been. Jonah discovered that Nineveh wouldn't be overturned, but you say it will be. Is Nineveh so much more wicked than we are? Does Yahweh treat them differently from us? Are we in the same danger as they are? Is it risky for us to rejoice in your message?

From Nahum of Elkosh
To Hilkiah ben Shallum, Priest in Jerusalem:

> 3:1Hey, town of bloodshed,
>> all of it deception,
> Full of plunder,
>> where prey doesn't depart.
> 2The sound of a whip,
>> the sound of the rumble of a wheel,
> A horse galloping,
>> a chariot jumping,
> 3Cavalry going up, sword flashing,
>> spear glittering, a multitude run through,
> A heap of carcases, no end of the corpses,
>> people collapse over their corpses.
>
> 4Because of the dimensions of the whore's whorings,
>> the well-favoured expert in charms,
> Who sells nations with her whorings,
>> kin-groups with her charms,
> 5Here am I towards you (a declaration of Yahweh
>> of Armies):
>> I shall expose your skirts over your face.
> I shall show the nations your nakedness,
>> kingdoms your slighting.
> 6I shall throw abominations over you,
>> demean you and make a spectacle of you;

[7]All who see you will flee from you,
and say, 'Nineveh is destroyed!
Who will mourn for her,
where shall I seek for people to comfort her?'

[18]Your shepherds have gone to sleep, king of Assyria;
your august people settle down.
Your people have scattered over the mountains,
and there's no one collecting them.
[19]There's no healing for your break;
your wound is severe.
All who hear the report of you
clap the palm of a hand at you,
Because to whom has bad fortune from you
not passed, continually? (3:1–7, 18–19)

Background and Foreground

How wise of the priests to raise those questions! And how subtle Nahum continues to be! Micah described Jerusalem as a city built on bloodshed (Micah 3:10), and "town of bloodshed" is the very expression that Ezekiel uses to describe Jerusalem (Ezekiel 22:2; 24:6). Ezekiel also speaks of Jerusalem whoring, as does Jeremiah (for example, Jeremiah 2:20; Ezekiel 16:30). The expressions Nahum uses provide good reason for Yahweh to take action against Nineveh. But the things that are true of Nineveh are also true of Jerusalem. And the visionary description of the conquest of Nineveh uses the same images as prophets use to describe the threatened conquest of Jerusalem. The same applies to the talk of shepherds failing in their duty and people scattered and the impossibility of healing. You can only rejoice in Yahweh putting down your imperial overlord if you don't share the empire's waywardness.

LETTERS TO HABAKKUK

While Nahum envisages the fall of Nineveh and the downfall of the Assyrian Empire, Habakkuk envisages, in parallel, the rise of Babylon and the Chaldeans, who were indeed the Assyrians' successors as the imperial power in the Middle East towards the end of the seventh century BC. Habakkuk itself takes the form of a dialog, like this book. So we will adapt Habakkuk's dialog with Yahweh and turn it into a dialog with Habakkuk.

A Letter to Habakkuk from Elishama ben Pelet

To my lord Habakkuk:

I belong to the clan of Issachar, in the north, but I live here in Jerusalem. My story is a complicated one. My ancestors had their land allocation near the city of Jezreel, where eventually King Ahab built his palace. I expect you know the story. Our land included a vineyard near the palace, and the king wanted to take over the land to use as the palace vegetable garden. He offered my ancestor Naboth an alternative plot of land. I would have agreed, but Naboth was apparently a stubborn guy and he wouldn't agree. So eventually the king fabricated some lie about Naboth placing a curse on him, managed to convince the elders it was true, got Naboth executed, and took over our land, so that our family ended up as sharecroppers. Which was ignominious, because having your own land is part of what makes it possible to hold your head high. But we managed; we had enough to eat.

Then in due course the Assyrians took over that entire region of Ephraim, which made my family feel that at least it was what the kings of Ephraim deserved. My family moved south to Samaria and became sharecroppers there. Then of course the Assyrians did it again. Again my family managed to get out rather than being taken off to Assyria as forced migrants. There are advantages to being peasants, you see: you can be on the move quickly! So they moved here from Samaria and started again. Here in Jerusalem, my great-great-grandfather got a job working for a potter and learned the trade, and it became the family trade, and we eventually inherited the potter's house. But now the king has decided he wants to extend his palace and he's evicting our family from the house. It's not as bad as what happened in Jezreel, but it's not so different.

I have to say it all makes it hard for me to believe in Yahweh as the God who is supposed to care about people being treated properly. How long am I supposed to cry out about such violence to Yahweh when he doesn't listen or rescue us? Why does he keep making my family watch the authorities treat us wrongly? Why is there no justice? Why does Yahweh simply let faithless people overwhelm faithful people?

From the prophet Habakkuk
To Elishama ben Pelet:

> 1:5Watch the nations,
> look, and be utterly astounded.

Because I'm going to do something in your days
    that you wouldn't believe when it was told.
⁶Because here am I, I'm going to raise up the
      Chaldeans,
    the bitter, quick-moving nation,
That goes to the far reaches of the earth,
    to possess dwellings that don't belong to it.
⁷It's terrible and fearful;
    from itself its authority and its dignity issue.
⁸Its horses are swifter than leopards,
    keener than wolves at evening;
Its steeds gallop;
    its steeds come from afar.
They fly like an eagle hastening to devour;
    ⁹all of it comes for violence.
The thrust of their faces is forwards;
    it gathers captives like sand.
¹⁰It derides kings,
    rulers are fun to it.
It makes fun of every fortress,
    it fortifies earth and captures it.
¹¹Then the wind sweeps on and passes through,
    and it becomes guilty, because its energy is
      its god. (1:5–11)

Background and Foreground

Yahweh's answer, then, is that he is going to cause the
Babylonians to come on Judah, and specifically on its tyrannical
leadership. "Chaldeans" (v. 6) is another term for Babylonians.
Chaldea is a region southeast of Babylon itself, but a Chaldean
dynasty ruled Babylon for a while and thus Chaldea came to
be a name for Babylon itself, a bit the way the Angles and the
Franks (who were both German!) gave their names to England
and France.

A Follow-Up to Habakkuk
from Elishama ben Pelet

To my lord Habakkuk:

But that won't do as a solution! I thought you were going to say something more moral than that! Using the Babylonians to bring trouble to the Judahite kings is no better than using the Assyrians to bring calamity on Ahaz and on Ephraim! It's going to mean more suffering for ordinary people, too. While I may think that the kings of Ephraim and Judah are faithless people, I'm beginning to believe that it's better to have them in charge than a Babylonian king. The Babylonians are just as bad as the Assyrians. They are people who are involved in bringing undeserved trouble to other peoples, like the Assyrians. They don't keep faith with people. They are merciless and ruthless in the way they operate in the world. How can Yahweh just stand there and watch them swallow other peoples? They resemble the fishermen in Lake Galilee, who throw out a huge dragnet and the fish all get caught in it and they die, and the fishermen then go home and celebrate. The Babylonians are like those fishermen, and we'll be the fish. I guess that's just the way superpowers are.

From the prophet Habakkuk
To Elishama ben Pelet:

> 2:3aBecause there's yet a vision about a set time,
> > it testifies about the end, and it won't
> > > deceive. . . .
> 4There, his appetite within him
> > is swollen, not upright,
> > whereas the faithful person will live by his
> > > truthfulness.
> 5How much more does wine betray

the arrogant man.
He won't abide,
   one who's let his appetite be as wide as Sheol.
The one who is like death,
   but he isn't full,
The one who gathers to himself all the nations,
   collects to himself all the peoples. . . .
6bHey, one who accumulates what's not his—
      how long,
   one who makes debts heavy for himself?
7Your creditors will suddenly arise, won't they,
   the people who make you tremble will
      wake up,
   and you will turn into plunder for them.
8Because you're one who despoiled many nations,
   all that's left of the peoples will despoil you,
On account of the human bloodshed and the
      violence against the country,
   the township and all the people who live in it.

9Hey, one who makes dishonest gain,
   a bad thing for his household,
To set his nest on high,
   to escape from the fist of bad fortune. . . .

12Hey, one who builds a town through bloodshed
   who establishes a township through evil. . . .

16bThe chalice in Yahweh's right hand
   will come round to you,
   with slighting in place of your splendour.

17Because your violence to Lebanon will cover you,
   your destruction of animals, which terrifies them,

> On account of human bloodshed and violence to
> the earth,
> the township and all who live in it. . . .
>
> [19a]Hey, one who says to wood, 'Wake up,'
> 'Get up,' to dumb stone,
> so it may teach. . . .
> [20]But Yahweh is in his sacred palace—
> be silent before him, all the earth.
> (2:3a, 4–9, 12, 16b–17, 19a, 20)

Background and Foreground

Yahweh grants Elishama's point and acknowledges that there must be a difference between the way he treats the person who is faithful and true and the way he treats people like the Babylonians. They will have their own comeuppance in due course, which they do when they get overwhelmed by the Persians after holding onto an empire for a relatively short time. In a neat image, Habakkuk likens the Babylonians to death itself, which is never satisfied with the number of people it has swallowed. It will be poetic justice: the ones who have plundered will become plunder; the ones who have done violence to nature (forest and animal) will be the victims of violence; the ones who thought they could turn to idols and didn't see they were giving commissions to things made of wood and stone will find themselves silent before the real God.

Another Follow-Up to Habakkuk
from Elishama ben Pelet

To my lord Habakkuk:

Yahweh in his sacred palace! In the heavens! All the earth to be silent before him! I feel put in my place. And if he is really

going to act, I'm happy to be put in my place. But what are
the implications regarding what Yahweh is like? Will he be
personally coming to sort things out in Judah? Where does he
come from? Have you seen Yahweh coming? What have you
seen? What will his arrival be like? Will it be like the exodus?
Will there be shaking like at Sinai?

And are you satisfied with that response from Yahweh?
How am I supposed to talk to Yahweh about it? When times
are tough (say, a person has been robbed of his vineyard, like
my ancestor Naboth, or thrown out of his house, as happened
to his family), how do we think about it? I know we can protest
to Yahweh. Is there anything else? Tell me how you would pray.

From the prophet Habakkuk
To Elishama ben Pelet:

> 3:3God comes from Teman,
>> the sacred one from Mount Paran. *(Rise)*
> His majesty has covered the heavens,
>> his praise has filled the earth.
> 4His brightness comes like dawn,
>> its rays from his hand,
>> and there is the hiding place of his vigour.
> 5Before him epidemic comes,
>> plague comes out at his feet.
> 6He has stood and shaken the earth;
>> he has looked, and agitated nations.
> Ancient mountains have shattered,
>> age-old hills sunk down.
> The age-old ways are his,
>> 7in place of the trouble that I have seen. . . .
> 8Are you wrathful at the Rivers, Yahweh,
>> is your anger at the Rivers,
>> is your wrath at the Sea,

When you mount on your horses,
 your chariots that bring deliverance?
⁹You totally bare your bow;
 your clubs are sworn, by your word. *(Rise)*
With the Rivers you split the earth;
 ¹⁰ᵃwhen they've seen you, mountains writhe.
A torrent of water has passed by,
 the Deep has given its voice. . . .
¹³ᵃYou have gone out for the deliverance of your
  people,
 for the deliverance of your anointed. . . .

¹⁷Because the fig tree may not bud,
 and there may be no produce on the vines,
The product of the olive may deceive,
 and the fields may not produce food,
Someone may cut off the flock from the fold,
 and there may be no cattle in the stalls:
¹⁸Yet I shall exult in Yahweh,
 rejoice in the God who delivers me.
¹⁹The Lord Yahweh is my resource,
 he makes my feet like the deer's,
  enables me to tread on the high places.
   (3:3–10a, 13a, 17–19)

Background and Foreground

Habakkuk's vision does picture Yahweh coming from Sinai, with the kind of reverberations and after-effects you might expect. It's awe inspiring and overwhelming and fearsome, but it means the deliverance of his people and their anointed king. And it means that they may experience calamity (the picture might imply the devastation an army invasion brings or a failure of the harvest) but it won't stop them exulting in Yahweh, because they know he is the God who delivers and that he will deliver in due course.

LETTERS TO ZEPHANIAH

The introduction to Zephaniah gives him a date, in broad terms: it's the time of King Josiah of Judah (640–609 BC), which means it's again approximately the same time period as Nahum and Habakkuk (and Jeremiah), the time when Assyria is declining and Babylon is on the rise. Josiah's reign saw a great reformation of Judah's religion (see 2 Kings 22–23), and Zephaniah's messages may imply the earlier part of that reign, when the reformation desperately needs to happen.

A Letter to Zephaniah from Gedaliah ben Amariah

To my lord Zephaniah ben Kushi:

Your grandfather here! I have to write to you about the state of religion in Jerusalem. You know that I lived most of my life through the dreadful reign of King Manasseh, may God not rest his soul, and King Amon wasn't much improvement. During that time, those of us who were appalled at the state of things in Jerusalem were advised to keep quiet.

You know how the Ephraimites were inclined to serve the traditional gods of Canaan at the traditional Canaanite shrines? Even with the best will in the world, it would have been hard to stop them. They had those two great national cathedrals in Dan and Beth-El, but the geographical size of Ephraim meant that most people were too far away to go there often. They were bound to go to those local shrines, and it would have been virtually impossible to control what went on there, even if anybody tried. In a strange way, we are fortunate in Judah that our country is so much smaller—at least, the area where most people live is smaller. Most people can get to Jerusalem if they want to, and the priests who live around the country could keep more control of what was going on in the local shrines.

All that changed with Manasseh. Maybe it was partly the people from Ephraim who came here after the fall of Samaria. Maybe another factor was that Manasseh felt under pressure to allow Assyrian religion to have an influence in Judah. Maybe another factor was that the people of Judah were just fed up with the way things were turning out in their life, as they had to pay such substantial taxes to the imperial center as well as to Jerusalem. And one way or another, Judah's relation with Yahweh went haywire.

But now the situation has changed in a direction that is potentially more positive. It turns out that Judah learned something else from Ephraim. It learned how to assassinate a king. So some people have gotten rid of Amon. I'm not exactly saying I approve of that. But I'm prepared to look on the bright side. And another bit of the bright side is that the Assyrians are in terminal decline. They've lost control of our end of their empire. So the people who have put little Josiah on the throne have the chance of cleaning up Judah's religion as well as its economics. The question is whether they will.

So what do you say, grandson? What do you think Yahweh has to say now?

From Zephaniah ben Kushi, son of Gedaliah
To Gedaliah ben Amariah:

> ^{1:4}I shall stretch out my hand against Judah,
>   and against all the inhabitants of Jerusalem.
> I shall cut off from this place
>   the remainder of the Master,
>   the names of the priestlings with the priests,
> ⁵The people who bow low on the roofs
>   to the army in the heavens,
> Who bow low, who swear, to Yahweh
>   and swear by Malkam,
> ⁶Who turn away from following Yahweh
>   and don't seek Yahweh nor inquire of him.
>
> ^{7a}Silence before the Lord Yahweh,
>   because Yahweh's Day is coming near. . . .
>
> ¹²At that time
> I shall search Jerusalem with lamps.
> I shall attend to the people
>   who are relaxing on their lees,
> Who are saying to themselves,
>   'Yahweh won't do something good and he
>   won't do something bad.'
> ¹³Their resources will be for plundering,
>   their houses will be for desolation.
> They will build houses but not live [there],
>   plant vineyards but not drink their wine. . . .
>
> ^{14b}The sound of Yahweh's Day is bitter;
>   the strong man is going to shriek there.
> ¹⁵That day will be a day of outburst,

151

> a day of pressure and distress,
> A day of desolation and devastation,
> a day of darkness and gloom,
> A day of cloud and shadow,
> [16]a day of horn blast and shout,
> Against the fortified towns,
> and against the lofty corner towers. . . .
> [17b]Their blood will be poured out like earth,
> their marrow like faeces. (1:4–7, 12–16, 17b)

> [2:3]Seek Yahweh, all you humble people in the country,
> who have implemented his ruling.
> Seek faithfulness, seek lowliness;
> perhaps you can hide on Yahweh's angry day.
> (2:3)

Background and Foreground

Zephaniah issues radical threats about Yahweh's Day as a dark time and not a time of blessing. They correspond to the threats of a prophet such as Amos and they also correspond to the warnings in the Torah, but they are applied to the particular context in Zephaniah's day. He focuses on Judah's religious faithlessness, which is also the focus of the actual reformation when it comes. Yahweh will deal with people's serving of the Master, Baal, down to the last vestige of it. He will deal with their reliance for guidance on the powers of the heavens, the stars and the planets, with Malkam their supposed "King." He will deal with their conviction that Yahweh will never do anything—he did nothing over the half-century of Manasseh's reign, did he? Zephaniah therefore summons people to turn to Yahweh.

There are some paradoxes in the way he issues his summons. When he talks to people who are "humble" (2:3), he sounds as if he is addressing ordinary people. But then he speaks of them as people who have seen to the implementing of government or authority. They are people with power. They are just claiming to be lowly in the sense of being submissive to Yahweh. And if they are people in power, what Zephaniah has already said makes it seem unlikely that they have been acting in that submissive way. So that's why he goes on to challenge them to be what they claim to be. They need to become faithful and lowly in relation to Yahweh. Then maybe they can escape the calamity that's coming.

A Follow-Up to Zephaniah from Gedaliah ben Amariah

To my lord Zephaniah ben Kushi:

That's fantastic and scary! It's just as well we know that Yahweh's devastating threats are as much a challenge to people to change as a declaration of intent. It's just as well that there is some possibility of Judah taking notice and reforming things. We do have more scope for reform now that Assyria is declining. Politically, we can get away with things we couldn't have got away with before. Maybe that's why Yahweh is making those declarations now. Maybe he was being long-tempered during Manasseh's time because the Assyrians were such a pressure on us. Now that things have changed politically, in a sense, paradoxically, it increases the pressure on us to change in the way we relate to Yahweh. But the people who put young Josiah on the throne and who are really going to be determining the country's policies—well, they had better take notice of the warnings you have been giving.

What about the broader politics? Assyria declining is excellent for us, but at the same time it introduces instability into what has been a stable political situation for my entire lifetime, as well as yours. What about the Philistines? They have been even more under Assyrian control than us, partly because they are down there on the coast and on the trade route from Mesopotamia to Egypt. As long as we have both been under Assyrian domination, we haven't been fighting each other. But over the centuries we used to fight. Sometimes we were stronger than they were, and sometimes they were stronger.

On the other side of the country, across the Jordan, Ephraim and Judah have always lived in tension with the Moabites and the Ammonites. Once the Assyrians are gone, we're going to be in dispute with them over land that had belonged to us. Some of it is land that Yahweh allocated to us back at the beginning.

And to the south, what will happen to our relationship with the Egyptians? They were ruled by the Sudanese until the Assyrians conquered Egypt, but when the Assyrians are gone, what will happen to Egypt? Of course, one would expect it to regain some of its old strength, so it will become potentially our new ally. But prophets like Isaiah used to warn us about getting involved with the Egyptians, just as much as he warned us about getting involved with the Assyrians. We were supposed to trust in Yahweh. That kind of question will arise again.

We are destined for interesting times. What do you think Yahweh has to say about that?

From Zephaniah ben Kushi, son of Gedaliah
To Gedaliah ben Amariah:

> 2:4Gaza will become abandoned,
>   Ashkelon a desolation.
> Ashdod will be dispossessed at midday,
>   Ekron uprooted. . . .
> 6The region by the sea will become abodes,
>   shepherds' cisterns, pens for flocks. . . .
> 8I have heard Moab's reviling,

the insults of Ammon, . . .
⁹ᵇMoab will become like Sodom,
   the Ammonites like Gomorrah: . . .
¹²You Kushites [Sudanese], too:
   run through by my sword.
¹³And he'll stretch out his hand against the north,
   and obliterate Assyria.
He'll make Nineveh a desolation,
   dry like the wilderness. . . .

³:¹Hey, rebellious and defiled one,
   oppressive town!
²It hasn't listened to a voice,
   it hasn't accepted correction.
It hasn't relied on Yahweh,
   it hasn't come near to its God.
³Its officials within it
   are roaring lions.
Its authorities are wolves at evening;
   they don't gnaw until morning.
⁴Its prophets are arrogant, people who break
         faith;
   its priests treat what's sacred as ordinary, they
         violate instruction.
⁵ᵃYahweh is faithful within it;
   he doesn't do evil. . . .

⁸ᵈBecause in my passionate fire
   the entire earth will be consumed.
⁹Because then I shall transform for the peoples
   purified speech,
So that all of them call on Yahweh's name,
   so that they serve him shoulder to shoulder.
      (2:4–6, 8, 9b, 12–13; 3:1–5a, 8d–9)

155

Background and Foreground

With hindsight, one can see that Zephaniah is here doing what anyone would expect if they've read Amos. First, he declares that Yahweh will deal with the peoples around Judah who might be a threat to it, who are Judah's present overlords, or who might seem plausible resources to it. And over subsequent decades, Judah did look to Egypt in this connection. So his words constitute a promise of protection, deliverance, and restoration, and also a warning about false reliance.

It's after those declarations against these other peoples that the parallel with Amos becomes significant, because the declarations turn out to lead into something about Jerusalem itself. When Zephaniah talks about other peoples, there are rather few comments about their wrongdoing—just that they have their eye on Judah's land and that they are overconfident and full of themselves. When Zephaniah comes to speak about Jerusalem's own wrongdoing, he has a lot more to say. He speaks of its resistance to listening to Yahweh's rebuke and correction and reliance on him, of the corruption of its leadership, of its unwillingness to see what he is doing when he puts down other peoples.

Maybe worse, Yahweh turns the other nations into the means of bringing disaster to Judah. And he will turn the nations themselves into worshipers of Yahweh.

Another Follow-Up to Zephaniah
from Gedaliah ben Amariah

To my lord Zephaniah ben Kushi:

Initially that was more encouraging than I expected, but the thing with Yahweh is, he never says what you would expect. Our neighbors are doomed, but so are we. And then, Yahweh is going to bring into being a vast new people to serve him, not Philistines and not Moabites or Ammonites and not Egyptians but also not Judahites?

In a sense, we couldn't complain. But in another sense we could, on the basis of something that has been implicit in your declarations about Jerusalem. Most Judahites are just ordinary people trying to get on with their farming and shepherding and parenting. It's the officials, the authorities, the prophets, the priests who are the real faithless people. The ordinary Judahites are more their victims. They don't deserve annihilation.

There's something else. Yahweh long ago made a commitment to us as a people and to our city. He didn't make that commitment because we had earned it. He just made it, despite what we were as much as because of what we were. Can he really just abandon us now? Hasn't he bound himself to us, even if we fail him? Isn't he like a father or mother who can't say that their children aren't their children anymore? He did say something like that to Hosea, but he also then raised a question about it.

Both those considerations point in another direction. Doesn't he owe it to himself, as well as to us, to resist the temptation to give up on us? Doesn't he owe it to himself and to us to take the kind of action that will do something about the forces that work for oppression and deception and self-confidence? Doesn't he owe it to himself and to us to bring encouragement and healing to the ordinary people who've lost out through the prosperity of the people who have power and ideas and energy that they have used for their own benefit?

From Zephaniah ben Kushi, son of Gedaliah
To Gedaliah ben Amariah:

> $3:11$On that day,
>> you [Jerusalem] won't be ashamed of all your
>> deeds,

with which you've rebelled against me.
Because then I shall remove from within you
  the people exulting in your majesty. . . .

¹²I shall leave remaining within you
  a humble, poor people,
  and they will find shelter in Yahweh's
    name. . . .
¹³ᶜBecause they are the ones who will pasture and
    lie down,
  with no one disturbing.

¹⁴Resound, Miss Zion,
  shout, Israel. . . .
¹⁵ᵇYahweh, Israel's King, is within you;
  you needn't be afraid of bad things
    anymore. . . .

¹⁶ᵇDon't be afraid, Zion;
  your hands shouldn't droop.
¹⁷Yahweh your God is within you,
  a strong man who delivers.
He'll celebrate over you with rejoicing,
  he'll hold his peace in his love,
  he'll be glad over you with resounding.
¹⁸The people who grieve on account of the set
    occasions—
  I'm gathering them from you;
  upon you they've been a burden, a reviling.
¹⁹Here am I, I'm going to deal with all your
    oppressors
  at that time.
I shall deliver the lame,
  collect the ones driven out.

I shall make them an object of praise and renown
whose shame was in the entire earth.

²⁰At that time I shall bring you—
yes, at the time I shall collect you.
Because I shall make you an object of renown and
praise
among all the peoples of the earth,
when I restore your fortunes before your eyes
(Yahweh has said). (3:11–20)

Background and Foreground

Gedaliah was right in both the points he made. Yahweh
says he will specifically deal with the leadership of the city,
people like politicians and pastors, the people who fail in
their ministry. On the other hand, he will look after the ordinary people. And yes, Yahweh can threaten to walk out on
Jerusalem, and he will eventually do so (and the city will fall
to the Babylonians), but he also promises to walk back in due
course. To put it another way, while he intends to abandon
them because of the way they treat another god as Malkam,
"their king," he promises that he will be present in the city as
"Israel's King." And forming a new worshiping people from
among the nations will not exclude doing things for Judah itself
that will make it an object of wonder.

LETTERS TO HAGGAI

Yahweh did walk out on Jerusalem in 587 BC and let the Babylonians destroy most of the city and devastate the temple. Then fifty years later the Persians put paid to the Babylonians, Yahweh did come back, and the Judahites began the task of restoring the temple. But there were conflicts among the groups who would like to be engaged in this project, and the work ceased for fifteen years. Then there was a new regime in Persia, and some leadership in relation to the temple was exercised by a Davidic prince, Zerubbabel; a priest, Jeshua; and two prophets, Haggai and Zechariah.

A Letter to Haggai from Joiakim ben Jeshua, Priest in Jerusalem

To my lord Haggai:

You know that my father appointed me project manager in connection with the temple restoration work here in Jerusalem and the work in the city more broadly. I came with him from Babylon when the Persians commissioned Judahites to go back to restore the temple (and to pray for the emperor there!). We did set the altar going again and my father made the offerings. People who hadn't been taken off to Babylon, or who had taken refuge in Ammon or somewhere and had crept back to Judah, had been praying in the hulk of the temple from time to time, but there were virtually no priests among them and they hadn't done anything to make proper worship possible again. They'd just left the temple in its devastated state. Until then, it would actually have been a bit dangerous to do anything to the devastation: I don't think the Babylonians would have been keen. It would have looked like an act of rebellion.

But we were now free to collect the stones from the altar and put them together and make some offerings to purify it (remember the Babylonian troops had done unmentionable things to it). And then, for the first time in fifty years, burnt offerings were made there as an expression of our commitment to Yahweh and in association with our prayers for Yahweh to come back there and be with us and help us with the restoring of the city—and protect us, actually. Although we had no need to worry about the Babylonians now, there were other peoples around who didn't think that our return was so wonderful an event.

The Persians had also given us a grant to cover the basic costs of the restoration work, so we were able to order cedar wood from Lebanon, the way Solomon did when he first built the temple. Down the seacoast it came, till it got to the River Yarkon and we could float it upstream, until we came to the hard bit of hauling the timber overland to Jerusalem itself. But it turned out that these logistics weren't our only problem. Some of those other peoples wanted to join in the building, and we were not sure that they were sufficiently committed to Yahweh for us to agree that they should. Then, when we said no, they turned the local Persian officials against us and made it impossible for us to continue the work.

But now there's a new administration in Persia after the deaths of Cyrus and Cambyses, and it seems to me that we could restart the work. But the problem is that people in Judah have other things on their minds, and you can't blame them. The Babylonians did a more thoroughgoing job of destroying the residential areas in the city than they did of the temple. It was easier—people's houses aren't made of the kind of stone that was used for the temple. All the roofs of people's houses were burnt, and so was anything made of manufactured brick. So people who came back, and could find where their family once lived, couldn't simply move back in and relax. They were squatting in ruins, and they're gradually trying to make their places habitable again. They have to do it in their spare time, while they're also commuting out into the farmland to try to grow enough to eat, or to work as laborers on other people's land. To make things even worse, the rains have been poor. The result is that people aren't starving, but they're not flourishing either.

So I'm stuck, and I'm wondering what Yahweh may be saying to us. Should we be practical and say, "Okay, let's suspend the work for a few more years till it becomes more feasible"? Or what?

From the prophet Haggai
To Joiakim ben Jeshua:

> 1:4Is it the time for you yourselves to live in your panelled houses, and this house lies waste? 5So now Yahweh of Armies has said this: 'Apply your mind to your ways. 6You've sown much but brought in little. You eat but without having enough. You drink but without getting drunk. You dress but without a person getting warm. And the people who earn wages earn them for a purse with holes. . . . 8Go up to the highland, bring wood and build the house, and I shall accept it and

find honour,' Yahweh has said. ⁹"You looked for much, but there—little. You brought it home, and I'd blow on it. On account of what (a declaration of Yahweh of Armies)? On account of my house that lies waste, and you're running each person to his own house. ¹⁰That's why the heavens above you have withheld dew, and the earth has withheld its produce, ¹¹and I've called for drought on the earth, on the mountains, on the grain, on the new wine, on the fresh oil, on all that the ground produces, on human beings, on animals and on all the labour of your fists." (1:4–6, 8–11)

Background and Foreground

It was a tough message, but sometimes Yahweh is like that. He is looking for an act of faith on their part. They will then have to wait and see what happens if they respond. . . .

Haggai, Zechariah, and Malachi especially love that title for God, "Yahweh of Armies." It can suggest bad news, but it can suggest good news. To this tiny colony under the control of the empire, it highlights the fact that the God of little Judah is the God with all power at his disposal.

A Letter to Haggai from Zerubbabel ben Shealtiel, Governor of Judah

To my lord Haggai:

First, I want to thank you for the way you received young Joiakim. Your message was challenging, but it was what people needed to hear, and it worked. It galvanized those of us who are involved in leadership who are a bit older than Joiakim and his generation. We could easily have said, "Let's wait for a while till the situation is easier," just as we did after we first came back fifteen years ago. But you said Yahweh would be with us, and he has been.

Unfortunately and paradoxically, the work itself has brought out into the open another form of discouragement. Anyone who is old enough to remember Solomon's temple would need to be about eighty years old. We have a handful of people of that age, and some of them are enthusiastic about the restoration work, but more of them remember how it used to be and think we can never replicate it. And of course they're right. The Babylonians pillaged anything from the temple that was worth pillaging. They didn't just take the gold and silver. They took the vast quantity of bronze and then burned whatever wasn't worth taking. The Persian administration has been generous with gold and silver and the wherewithal to buy cedar, and the ordinary people have been sacrificially generous too, but we're never going to be able to replicate Solomon's Temple. So it's a bit discouraging. Are we being too ambitious? Or not ambitious enough? Or what?

In addition, there are some people who keep reminding us that Yahweh originally commissioned a portable tent sanctuary, not a temple. And there are other people who remind us that building a temple was David's idea, not Yahweh's, and that even when Yahweh agreed to David's idea, he said, "Not this generation; leave it to the next generation." Yet other people remind us that Yahweh's actual palace is in the heavens and that the idea of him living in a palace made of stone doesn't make sense. He lives with people who are powerless and broken-hearted and trembling at his word. That's us, all right. If we aren't like that, no amount of temple building will make him live among us.

Will you consult Yahweh for us and see what he says? We need either to face the fact that we are undertaking something that is a mistake, or we need to take courage!

From the prophet Haggai
To Zerubbabel ben Shealtiel:

^{2:3}'Who among you remains who saw this house in its former splendour? How do you see it now? In comparison with it, it's just nothing in your eyes, isn't it. ⁴But now, be strong, Zerubbabel (Yahweh's declaration), be strong, Jeshua ben Jehozadaq, senior priest, be strong, all you people of the country (Yahweh's declaration). Act, because I am with you (a declaration of Yahweh of Armies), ⁵the thing that I solemnized with you when you got out of Egypt. My spirit stays among you. Don't be afraid.' ⁶Because Yahweh of Armies has said this: 'Once more, shortly, I'm going to shake the heavens and the earth, the sea and the dry land. ⁷I shall shake all the nations, and the things held in high regard belonging to all the nations will come. I shall fill this house with splendour (Yahweh of Armies has said). ⁸Mine is the silver and mine is the gold (a declaration of Yahweh of Armies). ⁹The splendour of this later house will be greater than the earlier one (Yahweh of Armies has said). In this place I shall give you well-being (a declaration of Yahweh of Armies).' (2:3–9)

Background and Foreground

So Zerubbabel got a straight answer to a straight question. It emphasizes that God is indeed "Yahweh of Armies" and that he does have all those resources at his disposal. Of course, those other voices that Zerubbabel quoted do affirm important principles. In Exodus, Yahweh did commission a portable sanctuary, 2 Samuel does record how it was David's idea to build the temple, and Isaiah 66 does remind people about where Yahweh really lives. But the principle of making something beautiful for God is also important, and so is Yahweh's willingness to come to live in a place that people build for him so that they can meet him there. Yahweh says, this is a moment to give priority to those principles.

A Follow-Up to Haggai from Zerubbabel ben Shealtiel, Governor of Judah

To my lord Haggai:

Sorry; it's me again. There's another group of people saying we have no need to put the effort into restoring the temple.

One of the points about the temple is that you go there to get cleansing when you've become taboo. So some people who get back from Babylon really appreciate the temple even in its unrestored state. They know they are defiled by having been in Babylon, because it was a land of false gods, and they can make a purification offering in the temple and find cleansing. Some other people who value that possibility are the people engaged in rebuilding work in the city. From time to time they find the remains of people who died in the siege of Jerusalem, and they are glad to give them a proper burial, but they are also glad that they can go and make a purification offering in the temple because they've been in contact with a dead person. Then there are the women who need to make a purification offering in connection with having a baby. And I'm most touched by the men who realize that they have done something morally wrong, like trying to cheat someone out of some land or out of some property that wasn't really theirs, or being unfaithful to their wives. They know they have to put that right with the owner or with their wife, but they know they also have to put it right with Yahweh, because they've taken his name in vain in the course of the transaction or in the course of making their marriage vows.

But there's that other group of people who think this is all superstition and that that's another reason why we have no need to put all this effort into the restoration of the temple. They think that what matters is that you repent and put things right with anyone you have wronged. You don't need a ritual as well. So that's another reason not to make restoring the temple a priority. We ought to be concerned with providing homes and food for the needy, not with irrational taboos.

What do you think?

From the prophet Haggai
To Zerubbabel ben Shealtiel:

> 2:11 Yahweh of Armies said this: 'Ask the priests for instruction, please: 12 "If someone carries sacred meat in the fold of his garment and touches bread or stew or wine or oil or any other food with the fold, does it become sacred?"' The priests answered, 'No.' 13 Haggai said: 'If someone who is taboo because of a body touches any of these, does it become taboo?' The priests answered: 'It becomes taboo.' 14 Haggai responded, 'So is this people, so is this nation before me (Yahweh's declaration) and so is the action of their hands. What they present there is taboo.
>
> 15 But now, apply your mind, please, from this day and onwards. Before the setting of stone on stone in Yahweh's palace, 16 from when these things happened, someone came to a twenty-measure heap, and there'd be ten; someone came to the wine vat to skim off fifty measures, there'd be twenty. 17 I struck you down with blight, with mildew, and with hail, in all the action of your hands, but you were not with me (Yahweh's declaration). 18 Apply your mind, please, from this day and onwards, from the twenty-fourth day of the ninth, from

the day when Yahweh's palace was founded. Apply your mind: ¹⁹is there still seed in the barn? Whereas until now the vine, the fig tree, the pomegranate, and the olive tree have not borne, from this day I shall bless.' . . .

²¹ᵇ'I'm going to shake the heavens and the earth, ²²overturn the throne of the kingdoms, destroy the strength of the nations' kingdoms, and overturn chariotry and its drivers. Horses and their riders will come down, each by his brother's sword.

²³On that day (a declaration of Yahweh of Armies), I shall take you, Zerubbabel ben Shealtiel my servant (Yahweh's declaration), and make you like a signet, because I've chosen you (a declaration of Yahweh of Armies).' (2:11–23)

Background and Foreground

So Yahweh's answer is: Yes, the questions about taboo and cleansing do matter. Those rules are not just superstition. They mean something to you, and they mean something to God, too. He likes his people to be cleaned up. So that's another reason why the restoration of the temple does matter (Hebrew doesn't have a word for "temple"; it calls the temple either Yahweh's "house" or his "palace").

If you want a bit more evidence that it's true, Haggai says, consider how much better you've done as you look back over this year compared with last year, now that you've been taking the restoration work seriously. Yahweh has kept his word, hasn't he?

Admittedly, there is another issue raised by Haggai's final promise. Yahweh has not done what the close of his words said. But maybe the fact that things are going so much better helps with that issue. Perhaps the juxtaposition of the reminder and the promise makes it possible to live with the unfulfilled promise. Yahweh has done one part of what he said, so hold onto the other part.

LETTERS TO ZECHARIAH

Zechariah ben Berechiah, the son of Iddo, was Haggai's contemporary in that context where people needed encouragement to get on with the restoration of the temple. Of all these twelve prophets, Zechariah is the one to whom Yahweh gave the most visions, so Yahweh's responses to people's "letters" to Zechariah often come in picture form. They thus make people think and wonder.

The second half of the Zechariah scroll, however, takes the form of enigmatic promises without any time references, and it's not clear whether we are supposed to take them as from Zechariah or from a later prophet, whose own name we don't know. In connection with them, I just refer to "the prophet" but treat them as if they come from a later period within Zechariah's lifetime. The only concrete information we have on issues that they might then need to address comes from Isaiah 56–66, from the books of Ezra and Nehemiah, and from Malachi. They seem to include many references to events in the prophet's day, but we don't know what these events were. So many elements in these prophecies remain puzzling.

A Letter to Zechariah from Jeshua ben Jehozadaq, Senior Priest

To my lord Zechariah ben Berechiah:

I am grateful to you for the way your colleague Haggai has encouraged my son in his responsibility as project manager for the work on the temple and my brother Zerubbabel in his leadership of the community. Now I have a troubling question of my own that I will put to you.

In my grandfather Seraiah's day, Jeremiah said that Babylonian control of Judah would last seventy years and that the Judahites who were taken to Babylon as forced migrants with King Jehoiachin would come back then. I'm not sure whether to call those words of Jeremiah a threat or a promise; perhaps they were both. They meant that the people's exile wasn't going to last a short time, but they also meant that it wasn't going to last forever. And I don't think Jeremiah meant seventy years as opposed to sixty-nine or seventy-one. The figure was a way of suggesting a long but limited period of time. In the event, a bit less than seventy years actually passed to when Babylon fell. But Jeremiah also implied that the end of the seventy years would see the end of affliction and its replacement by well-being. He promised a future characterized by hope. When Cyrus told us we could come home and gave us resources to help us restore the temple, we thought that this time of complete fulfillment had come. We were stupid, really. We hadn't seen how the thing that had actually happened was the replacement of one imperial power by another. We're still a colonial people; we're just under a different superpower, Persia instead of Babylon. And the tough side to the past fifteen years since we came back has underlined that fact.

To put it another way, if one takes "seventy" as a precise number and starts the seventy years from the final fall of

Jerusalem, they aren't quite over yet—they'll be over in a couple of years. And in our community experience, too, the seventy years don't really seem to be over yet. So my question is, how are we to understand Yahweh's promise? What is he doing with us and with the superpowers? Are we to look forward to the completion of seventy years from the fall of Jerusalem? Will that be Yahweh's Day arriving?

From the prophet Zechariah ben Berechiah
To Jeshua ben Jehozadaq:

1:7bYahweh's word came to Zechariah ben Berechiah, son of Iddo:

8I saw by night: there, a man riding on a red horse. He was standing among myrtle trees that were in the deep. Behind him were red, brown, and white horses. 9I said, 'What are these, my lord?' The envoy who was speaking with me said, 'I'll show you what those are.' 10The man who was standing among the myrtle trees answered, 'These are ones that Yahweh sent to go round in the earth.'

11They answered Yahweh's envoy who was standing among the myrtle trees, 'We've been going round in the earth. There, the entire earth is living quiet.'

12Yahweh's envoy answered, 'Yahweh of Armies, how long will you not have compassion on Jerusalem and on Judah's towns, which you have been condemning these seventy years?' 13Yahweh answered the envoy who was speaking with me with good words, comforting words.

14The envoy who was speaking with me said to me, 'Call out: "Yahweh of Armies has said this: 'I have felt a great passion for Jerusalem and for Zion, 15and I—I have been feeling a great fury with the nations that are peaceful, because I was a bit furious, but they helped it become bad fortune.' ¹⁶Therefore Yahweh has said this: 'I'm turning back to Jerusalem in compassion. My house will be built up in it (a declaration of Yahweh of Armies), and a cord will be stretched over Jerusalem.'" ¹⁷Call out further: "Yahweh of Armies has said this: 'My towns will again flow with good things. Yahweh will again comfort Zion and again choose Jerusalem.'"" (1:7b–17)

Background and Foreground

The Persian Empire was the biggest empire that the Middle East had known, and its emperor had a distinctively organized and clever system for keeping tabs on what was happening throughout his empire. His horsemen patrolled around the empire and reported back to the center. Yahweh pictures himself having an equivalent system for knowing what is happening in his own bigger empire. What they report is that everything is quiet. This peacefulness is not the good news that it sounds, because Judah wants Yahweh to disturb things, to put down the empire and restore his own people's independence. Yahweh's envoy (one of the supernatural beings traditionally referred to as angels) presses Yahweh concerning this matter on Judah's behalf, and Yahweh promises that he will take action. It will express both compassion and passion for Judah, as well as anger with the imperial powers. But he doesn't say anything more specific about the timeframe.

A Letter to Zechariah from Joiakim ben Jeshua, Senior Priest

To my lord Zechariah ben Berechiah:

I think you know that I am project manager for the rebuilding and restoration work in Jerusalem. I have consulted helpfully with Haggai concerning matters to do with the temple, but I have a question about the city more broadly.

Although the temple restoration has certain kinds of problems attached to it, the dimensions of the project are basically set. With the rebuilding of the city, it's more complicated. You know that the Babylonians demolished the old wall around the city. The basic wall goes back to the Jebusites, though King David reinforced it and King Solomon pushed it farther north in connection with building the temple. King Hezekiah later extended it westwards, as the city had grown by his day, but even that extension didn't include all the city's homes. The question we have to decide at the moment is, how big should the city be now?

Like any proper city, it needs walls. It's partly a pride thing. But it's also a practical thing. The empire is pretty settled now, but who knows what the future will bring? We do know that relations with the other peoples that live around Judah are not very friendly. Who knows how things will turn out in the future?

So everybody's agreed that we need walls. As far as dimensions are concerned, there is a realistic school of thought that points out that not many people live in Jerusalem now, and it's not just because it's in such a mess. Most people who settled in Babylon or elsewhere have no desire to come back to this little out-of-the-way city. And the people whose families moved to live in nearby places like Mizpah are happy there. They're not going to be coming back, either. So (this school of thought says) make it as small as you can. A middle-of-the-road school of thought calls this an act of terrible unfaith. The foundations of Hezekiah's wall are still there; the Babylonians only destroyed the superstructure. Let's restore that as the city's dimensions. An even more visionary school of thought says: If the city extended west and north before, let's have it do so again!

What do you think? Does Yahweh have anything to say to us about the question, or does he want us to use our common sense?

From Zechariah ben Berechiah
To Joiakim ben Jeshua:

1:18I lifted my eyes and looked: there, four horns. 19I said to the envoy who was speaking with me, 'What are these?' He said to me, 'These are the horns that scattered Judah, Israel, and Jerusalem.' 20And Yahweh showed me four smiths. 21I said, 'What are these coming to do?' He said, 'These are the horns that scattered Judah to such an extent that no one lifted his head. But these [the smiths] have come to disturb them by throwing down the horns of the nations that lifted a horn against the country of Judah, to scatter it.'

2:1I lifted my eyes and looked: there, a man with a measuring line in his hand. 2I said, 'Where are you going?' He said to me, 'To measure Jerusalem, to see exactly what is its breadth and its length.' 3But there, the envoy who was speaking with me was going out, and another envoy was going out to meet him. 4He said to him, 'Run, speak to that young man: "Jerusalem will be inhabited as unwalled villages because of the number of people and animals within it. 5And I myself shall be for it (Yahweh's declaration) a wall of fire round, and I shall be splendour within it."'

6'Hey, hey, flee from the northern country (Yahweh's declaration), because I'm scattering you like the four winds of the heavens (Yahweh's declaration).' 7Hey, Zion, escape, you who live in Miss Babylon. 8Because Yahweh of Armies has said this (after splendour sent me) regarding the nations who plundered you: the one touching you was touching the apple of his eye. 9'Because here am I, I'm going to shake my hand against them. They will become spoil for their servants.' And you will acknowledge that Yahweh of Armies sent me.

¹⁰'Resound, rejoice, Miss Zion, because here am I—I'm coming to dwell within you (Yahweh's declaration). ¹¹Many nations will attach themselves to Yahweh on that day and will become my people, and I shall dwell within you.'

And you will acknowledge that Yahweh sent me to you. ¹²And Yahweh will have Judah as his domain on the sacred ground, and will again choose Jerusalem.

¹³Hush, all flesh, before Yahweh, because he has roused himself from his sacred abode. (1:18–2:13)

Background and Foreground

Joiakim needs to see how significant his work is. An animal's horn is the embodiment of its strength. Four horns suggest the four points of the compass and thus the entire world, or at least the world empire. Paradoxically but profoundly, the smiths or craftsmen who are rebuilding Jerusalem and its temple are bringing the empire down by their work. On the other hand, Joiakim needs to see the danger in thinking that he can calculate how big the city of God should be and the folly in thinking that he needs to worry about its protection.

And if he's worried about whether he will have the resources for the work, he needs to overhear Yahweh disturbing the Judahites who are still in Babylon and promising to take action on Jerusalem's behalf. He's speaking of a new kind of scattering, not a negative one like the one that spread Judahites all over the world in exile but a positive one that scatters them from all over Babylonia back to Jerusalem.

Jerusalem is to rejoice at the fact that Yahweh intends to come to live in the city again, through the restoration of the temple, and that nations will come to join Judah as part of Yahweh's people. As Habakkuk urged the whole world to be silent before Yahweh, Zechariah urges all flesh to do so. This exhortation is more positive. All flesh is going to be able to recognize that

Yahweh has taken action in connection with the restoration of the temple and that he is accessible to everyone there.

Another Letter to Zechariah from Jeshua ben Jehozadaq, Senior Priest

To my lord Zechariah ben Berechiah:

I need to write to you about something more personal. I have to acknowledge that when we were away from Jerusalem, it was difficult to avoid being affected by the impurity of life in Babylon. It's not that Babylon is impure because Yahweh isn't there, as if he were not the God of the whole world; I know he is. And it's not that he was absent from Babylon in particular, though I know my father initially thought he might be willfully absent because we were under his discipline; but he appeared to a prophet like Ezekiel there and he spoke to us. But it was hard to avoid the impurity of association with other so-called gods in Babylon. At least, it was hard for members of the priesthood like my father and then me, because the Babylonians expected us to take part in their festivals. We had to go through the motion of cheering when the great statue of Marduk was carried through the streets.

And people who were with us in Babylon know we did that. They could avoid it if they wished, because they were laypeople, and they thought that somehow we should be able to avoid it. But we couldn't, or at least we didn't. And now they say that we are too compromised—that I am too compromised—to be engaged in leadership and priestly ministry here in Jerusalem. We need to give way to a generation who are not compromised.

So I have a question about the way I look at myself. Should I accept that I can never be clean, never be purified from the effect of what we had to do? And therefore should I accept that I should resign my position? I can live with that, if it is Yahweh's will. It would be a bit like accepting that one has a skin disease ["leprosy"] and knowing that one has to be careful of affecting other people and thereby making it impossible for them to go into the temple. In an analogous way, maybe I am in danger of making the whole temple and its services impure. But if the answer is that I can be cleansed, I then have another concern, about how the community looks at me. If I am to continue in my ministry, I need Yahweh to make that clear to them as well as to me.

From Zechariah ben Berechiah
To Jeshua ben Jehozadaq:

3:1He showed me Jeshua the senior priest standing before Yahweh's envoy, and the adversary standing at his right to act as his adversary. 2Yahweh said to the adversary, 'Yahweh reprimand you, adversary, Yahweh who chose Jerusalem reprimand you. Isn't this a burning stick snatched from the fire?' 3 Jeshua was wearing filthy clothes as he was standing before the envoy.

4He avowed to the beings who were standing before him, 'Take the filthy clothes off him,' and he said to him, 'Look: I've made your waywardness pass on from you, and you may wear fine robes. 5And I've said, "They should put a pure turban on his head."' They put the pure turban on his head and dressed him in clothes as Yahweh's envoy was standing by.

6Yahweh's envoy testified against Jeshua: 7'Yahweh of Armies has said this: "If you walk in my ways and keep my charge, you yourself will both judge my house and also keep watch on my courtyards, and I shall give you movement among these who are standing in attendance. ⁸Listen, please, Jeshua, senior priest, you and your fellows who are sitting before you, because they are people who constitute a sign. Because here am I, I'm going to bring my servant, Branch. ⁹Because here's the stone that I've put before Jeshua. On one stone are seven eyes. Here am I, I'm going to make its engraving (a declaration of Yahweh of Armies), and I shall remove this country's waywardness in one day.

¹⁰On that day (a declaration of Yahweh of Armies) you will call, each person his neighbour, under his vine and under his fig tree."' (3:1–10)

Background and Foreground

Zechariah pictures Jeshua as on trial in the heavenly court before Yahweh and his envoys or aides, with "the adversary" (3:1) as the prosecuting attorney (the word for "adversary" is *satan*, but that's an ordinary Hebrew word and we shouldn't read "Satan" into Zechariah's words). Yahweh as the president of the court throws the case out. It's not that the charges have no basis. It's that Yahweh thinks it's more important to see Jeshua as someone miraculously rescued from the fire than to focus on the smell of the fire on him. Yahweh is therefore prepared to do any miraculous cleansing of Jeshua that's needed so he can function as priest.

It doesn't mean Jeshua can be casual about his commitment to Yahweh. While in one sense it's no more important for him to walk in Yahweh's ways than it is for a layperson, his laxness would have bigger implications for him as a minister and for his people. If he does walk in Yahweh's ways, he will have the same sort of access to the heavenly court itself as a prophet has. Further, there is actually something miraculous about the fact that the company of priests have been able to commence their work again in Jerusalem. They are a sign that Yahweh is not finished with Jerusalem. More on what they are a sign of will become clearer in the visions that follow.

A Letter to Zechariah from Zerubbabel ben Shealtiel Governor of Judah

To my lord Zechariah ben Berechiah:

I have consulted your colleague Haggai about the pressures of my responsibility here in Jerusalem, and I apologize for troubling you as well, but your vision about Jeshua encourages me to do so. The obstacles to our completing the restoration of the temple and the city really are huge. The mountain of rubble that we have to clear away is a kind of symbol of the project itself. And we can't forget that it is also a symbol of the suffering our grandparents and great-grandparents went through when the Babylonians destroyed the city and devastated the temple.

Then there are the conflicts among the people here within the city, which Jeshua talked about. And there are conflicts involving the people around, Judahites who never went to Babylon and people who claim to acknowledge Yahweh but whose allegiance we're not sure about. There are conflicts with people who claim to represent the Persian administration, who stopped us getting on with the rebuilding for years. I spend a lot of time trying to mend fences with some of these people or standing firm with others of them. It's all an obstacle to getting the work done. Then there are the people who think that the Davidic line is hopelessly compromised by the history of the kings over the years that led up to the fall of Jerusalem and who aren't necessarily convinced that they should accept my leadership.

But what I keep coming back to is simply the size of the

project. I mean, it was all very well for Solomon with all those conscript workers from the nations around, and it was all very well earlier for David when he had become someone upon whose word people would do things at the drop of a hat, yes sir, so sir, three bags full, sir. Nobody says "Yes sir" to me. Nobody apart from Haggai calls me "governor."

From Zechariah ben Berechiah
To Zerubbabel ben Shealtiel:

> 4:1The envoy who was speaking with me came back and woke me up like someone who wakes up from his sleep. 2He said to me, 'What are you looking at?' I said, 'I looked, and there—a candelabrum of gold, all of it, with its bowl on top of it, and its seven lamps on it, seven spouts each for the lamps that were on top of it, 3and two olive trees by it, one to the right of the bowl and one to its left.' 4I avowed to the envoy who was speaking with me, 'What are these, my lord?' 5The envoy who was speaking with me answered me, 'Don't you know what these are?' I said, 'No, my lord.' 6He answered me. . .

>> 'This is Yahweh's word to Zerubbabel: "Not by resources, not by energy, but by my spirit," Yahweh of Armies has said. 6Who are you, big mountain, before Zerubbabel? Into flatland. He will take out the top stone, with shouts of "Grace, grace to it!"'

>> 8Yahweh's word came to me: 9'Zerubbabel's hands have founded this house and his hands will finish it off.' And you will acknowledge that Yahweh of Armies sent me to you. 10Because who despises the day of little things?

They will rejoice when they see the metal stone
in Zerubbabel's hand.

. . . 'These seven are Yahweh's eyes ranging through the
entire earth.' [11]I avowed to him, 'What are these two
olive trees on the right of the candelabrum and on its
left?' [12]And I avowed to him a second time, 'What are
the two ears [of grain] of the olive trees that pour out
gold from themselves by means of the two gold pipes?'
[13]He said to me, 'Don't you know what these are?' I said,
'No, my lord.' [14]He said, 'These are the two sons of fresh
oil who stand by the Lord of the entire earth.' (4:1–14)

Background and Foreground

So both the leaders of the community need their position
bolstered, because of the dimensions of their task or because
of their own fretfulness or because of people's opposition
to them or their doubts about them. Here Yahweh offers
encouragement for them both, such as might also boost their
standing in other people's eyes when they hear what Yahweh
is saying about them. You know how the candelabrum in the
temple will need an oil supply? And you know how it shines
out, giving light? Well, the candelabrum stands for Yahweh's
light shining out. It is destined to shine out over the whole
world. And Zerubbabel and Jeshua are the olive trees pro-
ducing the oil for the candelabrum. They make its shining
possible by their work on the temple and in the temple. So,
Zerubbabel, don't be put off by the mountain of rubbish. It
will go. The work will get done, not because you have the
energy but because Yahweh's spirit working in you has the
energy. Then, if we may read the previous vision and this
one in light of each other, the stone in that vision will be the
capstone of the temple building (the metal stone is a construc-
tion tool).

A Follow-Up to Zechariah from Jeshua ben Jehozadaq, Senior Priest

To my lord Zechariah ben Berechiah:

I have been thinking about Yahweh's promise to me that he would remove the country's waywardness in a single day. I want to put in a plea to Yahweh about that promise. The work that Zerubbabel and I are doing to rebuild the city is all very well, but there is another kind of restoration work that it needs. I have had to face up to the way I was stained by being too close to Babylon's so-called gods. But I wasn't the only one, and lots of Judahites in Babylon were quite happy to turn to Marduk. After all, they would say, he defeated Yahweh in 587, didn't he? It's not so different in Jerusalem now. In my great-grandfather's day, there were people in Jerusalem who looked for guidance to heavenly powers, and that sort of thing was a major reason why Yahweh walked out on the city. And I'm not so naïve as to assume that nobody thinks that way any longer. So there is waywardness that I need to take a lead in combating, but unless Yahweh fulfils the kind of promises that he made through Jeremiah and Ezekiel, about a change in people's attitudes, my attempts to clean things up will get nowhere.

I'm concerned about faithfulness in people's relationships with one another as well as faithfulness in their relationship with Yahweh. In my great-grandfather's day, people knew where their house was in Jerusalem because they were living in it, and they knew which was their land because they were growing their food there, though even that didn't stop unscrupulous people cheating simple people out of their land. Three generations later, the situation is impossible. Squatters came to live in the ruins in Jerusalem and repaired them a bit and now they say the houses are theirs. Then a family comes back from

Babylon and says, "That's our house." How do you know if it's true? The Babylonian administration told needy people to go and grow their food on abandoned land, and they did and they come to regard it as their land. Then a family comes back and says, "That's our land." How do you know if it's true?

From Zechariah ben Berechiah
To Jeshua ben Jehozadaq:

5:1I again lifted my eyes and looked—there, a flying scroll. 2He said to me, 'What are you looking at?' I said, 'I'm looking at a flying scroll. Its length is ten metres and its width five metres.' 3He said to me, 'This is the vow that's going out over the face of the entire country. Because everyone who steals (from this side, according to it) has gone free of guilt, and everyone who swears (from the other side, according to it) has gone free of guilt. 4I'm causing it to go out (a declaration of Yahweh of Armies) and it will come into the thief's house and the house of the person who swears by my name for falsehood. It will lodge inside his house and consume it, both its timbers and its stones.'

5The envoy who spoke with me went out and said to me, 'Lift up your eyes, please, and look. What's this going out?' 6I said, 'What is it?' He said, 'This is the barrel that's going out.' And he said, 'This is their appearance in the entire country.' 7And there, a lead disk lifted, and it was a woman sitting inside the barrel. 8He said, 'This is Faithlessness.' He thrust her inside the container and thrust the lead disk to its mouth.
9I lifted my eyes and looked, and there—two women going out with wind in their wings (they had wings like a stork's wings). They carried the barrel between the earth and the heavens. 10I said to the envoy who was

speaking with me, 'Where are they making the container go?' [11]He said to me, 'To build it a house in the country of Shinar, which will be established, and it will be settled down there on its established place.' (5:1–11)

Background and Foreground

The flying scroll makes one think of the Torah, which lays down the law about matters such as honesty and land, matters that are vital to people's lives, and promises that trouble will come to people who ignore the obligations of the covenant. The problem is people being acquitted when they have actually stolen and lied in court. Yahweh promises that the Torah will do its work: he will ensure that trouble comes to guilty people. Then there is Faithlessness, which has its eye on people throughout the country. Yahweh promises that faithlessness will be taken to where it belongs; Shinar is another name for Babylon. It may not be significant that the personification of faithlessness is specifically a woman, any more than that the person who accuses Jeshua is a man. But it is noteworthy that it is also female figures who are disposing of the barrel. And its being a woman might mean the vision would come across as a taunt to the men in the community who are inclined to pray to other gods or to marry women who pray to other gods.

A Letter to Zechariah from Josiah
ben Zephaniah, Craftsman

To my lord Zechariah ben Berechiah:

I am a craftsman in precious metal. It has been my family's work for generations. They worked in this way in Jerusalem in the old days, making jewelry for people—making necklaces and rings. They also looked after the maintenance of the gold and silver items in the temple. The Babylonians, of course, took off all the craftsmen, and my family got work of that kind in Babylon. One of the worst and best things about it was that we got the job of looking after the things from the temple that the Babylonians also took there and put in the treasuries of their own gods. But at least we knew where they were, and we could dream of being able to bring them back one day. Of course, I was born in Babylon, and my father taught me the craft. Then we leaped at the chance to come back to Jerusalem and join in the restoration project. So we brought the things from the temple back with us and we've been making them ready for when the restoration work is complete. And in addition, there was quite a lot of gold and silver donated by Judahites in Babylon who couldn't come back for some reason. Some of them were too old or frail, or they were too settled and doing too well and didn't want to come back, but they had a bit of a bad conscience. So they made a donation.

We managed to find the family's old workshop in the city, in the base of our old house, which was so devastated that not even squatters had bothered with it. We had to spend a lot of time making it habitable, but we were also looking forward to being able to do the work on the things from the temple. And already people were starting to get married and needing rings and necklaces and bracelets.

Then an odd thing happened. Three new arrivals from Babylon showed up, with more gold and silver as gifts for Yahweh's work. They said I had to make a double crown, a circle of silver and a circle of gold. It was ultimately for Zerubbabel, our governor. He's a descendant of David, so he qualifies to be king, but nobody wants to imply that we're making him king (at the moment!). You know the trouble we got into fifteen years ago just because we started rebuilding the temple! We don't want to risk antagonizing the local Persian administration, let alone the emperor, who has had to deal with rebellions in different parts of his empire. But these three men, Helday, Tobiah, and Yedaiah, said we were to inform you that they had come with this commission and ask what we were all supposed to do next.

From Zechariah ben Berechiah
To Josiah ben Zephaniah:

6:1I lifted my eyes again and looked, and there—four chariots going out from between two mountains; the mountains were mountains of copper. 2In the first chariot the horses were red, in the second chariot the horses were black, 3in the third chariot the horses were white, in the fourth chariot the horses were dappled, strong.

4I avowed to the envoy who was speaking with me, 'What are these, my lord?' 5The envoy answered me, 'These are the four winds of the heavens, going out after standing by the Lord of the entire earth.' 6The one where the black horses are—they were going out to the northern country. The white left after them. The dappled went out to the southern country. 7So the strong went out. When they sought to go, so as to go about through the earth, he said, 'Go, go about through the earth.' So they went about through the earth. 8He cried out to me and spoke to me: 'Look, the ones going out to the northern country have settled my spirit in the northern country.'

9Yahweh's word came to me: 10'Receive from the exile community, from Helday, from Tobiah, and from Yedaiah, and you yourself are to come on that day, to come to the house of Josiah ben Zephaniah, when they've come from Babylon:—11you're to receive gold and silver and make crowns and put them on the head of Jeshua ben Jehozadaq the senior priest, 12and say to him, "Yahweh of Armies has said this: 'There is the man whose name is Branch. From his place he will branch out and build Yahweh's palace. [13]He's the one who'll build Yahweh's palace. He's the one who'll put on majesty, and sit and rule on his throne. A priest will be by his throne, and there'll be peaceful counsel between the two of them. [14]For Helem, for Tobiah, for Yedaiah, and for Hen ben Zephaniah, the crowns will be a memorial in Yahweh's palace. [15]Distant people will come and build in Yahweh's palace, and you will acknowledge that Yahweh of Armies sent me to you. It will happen if you really do listen to the voice of Yahweh your God.'"' (6:1–15)

Background and Foreground

The two mountains stand for Yahweh's dwelling in the heavens, and the horses and chariots go out like the wind or go out empowered by Yahweh's breath/wind/spirit to the four corners of the world to implement Yahweh's will there. Except that they are not focused on all four corners of the world. In the account of the four winds in the vision, the punch line comes where a punch line usually comes, at the end. The northern country is Babylon, where many Judahites still live. Yahweh is not especially satisfied with the fact that they are content to stay there. But now his aides are settling his spirit there.

The story that follows relates a result. Zechariah is to get Josiah to make a double crown with the gold and silver that has been brought by the three men Josiah wrote about. The double crown is in due course to go on the head of Zerubbabel, the rebuilder of the temple (again it's referred to as Yahweh's palace). So now we know the answer to the question left over from Zechariah's vision about Jeshua's own restoration. Here, although the crown will go on Jeshua's head, it's really Zerubbabel's crown. Perhaps it's to be a vicarious crowning rather than an actual crowning of Zerubbabel himself, because of the danger Josiah refers to. But Zerubbabel is the man who is the branch from David. Yahweh doesn't say he'll be king. But he will sit on a throne. . . .

A Letter to Zechariah from Sar-Ezer and Regem-Melek of Beth-El

To our lord Zechariah ben Berechiah:

You will recognize that our names are Babylonian, like Zerubbabel's, and like him we belong to families that came back to Judah when we were free to do so. In our case, the remains of our extended families that had not been forced to migrate had abandoned Jerusalem when the Babylonians destroyed our house, and they had settled in Beth-El. So that's why we went back there.

Over the years, the people in Beth-El have been among the ones grieving and fasting for decades about the destruction of Jerusalem and the devastation of the temple, and the members of our family have naturally taken part in the mourning and fasting. On some of the regular fasting occasions they would come to Jerusalem to join in services in the temple courtyard. They would use the prayers in Lamentations to express the community's grief. They could walk to Jerusalem during the morning, spend several hours at the temple, and walk back before dark.

So we've been joining them. Yet now the situation seems to be changing. You people in Jerusalem restored the altar. You started the rebuilding work. You had a great celebration. We know you then had to stop, but now you've started again. So the people of Beth-El have asked us to inquire of you whether the time for fasting is over. It seems that their prayers are in the midst of being answered. Or would that be taking too much for granted? Given what happened after the work first got started, should we keep praying and keep fasting?

There might be some other questions about fasting that we should ask you to comment on. When Israel had great festivals of praise in the past, it could be for Yahweh's sake, but it could be for the worshipers' sake, because they had a great time. And we too have been wondering whether, paradoxically, there is an equivalent danger about fasting and mourning. Maybe it's also self-indulgence. It gives us the means of expressing our sadness, for our own sake. We let it all hang out. It makes us feel better. There's something even more worrying. There was lots of fasting in Jerusalem in Jeremiah's day, but he was quite cynical about it. As he saw it, there was a mismatch between people's mourning and their celebrating, and their everyday lives. So what does Yahweh think about fasting and prayer?

From Zechariah ben Berechiah
To Sar-Ezer and Regem-Melek:

7:4 A word from Yahweh of Armies came to me: 5 "Say to all the people of the country and to the priests, "When you fasted and lamented in the fifth and in the seventh even these seventy years, did you really fast for me? 6 When you eat and when you drink, it's you who eat and you who drink, isn't it? 7 They're the words that Yahweh called out by means of the earlier prophets, aren't they, when Jerusalem was peopled and peaceful, and its towns round it, and the Negeb and the Lowland were peopled? . . . 9 Exercise truthful authority, exercise commitment and compassion each person with his brother. 10 Don't oppress widow and orphan, alien and humble. Don't think up bad dealings each person against his brother in his mind." [11]But they refused to heed and presented a defiant shoulder. They stopped their ears from listening. [12]They made their mind concrete so as not to listen to the instruction and the words that Yahweh of Armies sent by his spirit by means of the earlier prophets, and great wrath came from Yahweh of Armies. [13]As he called but they didn't listen, "so they'll call and I shall not listen," Yahweh of Armies said. [14]"And I blasted them away to all the nations that they hadn't known. The country was desolate behind them from anyone passing through or coming back. They made a country that was held in high regard into a desolation."' . . .

[8:2]'Yahweh of Armies has said this: "I feel a great passion for Zion. I feel a fierce passion for it." [3]Yahweh has said this: "I'm coming back to Zion and I shall dwell within Jerusalem. Jerusalem will be called 'Truthful Town,' and the mountain of Yahweh of Armies 'Sacred Mountain.'"

[4]Yahweh of Armies has said this: "Old men and old women will again sit in Jerusalem's squares, each with his cane in his hand because of the great number of his days. [5]The town's squares will be full of boys and girls having fun in its squares."

[6]Yahweh of Armies has said this: "Because it will be fantastic in the eyes of the remainder of this people in those days, will it also be fantastic in my eyes (a declaration of Yahweh of Armies)?"

[7]Yahweh of Armies has said this: "Here am I, I'm going to deliver my people from the eastern country and from the western country, [8]and bring them, and they will dwell within Jerusalem. They will be a people for me and I shall be God for them, in truth and faithfulness."' (7:5–8:8)

Background and Foreground

Initially, Yahweh's response is ominous and discouraging; it confirms the hunches of the people asking the question. Fortunately, Yahweh doesn't stop there. There's a passion about Yahweh's exhortation, his critique, and his reminder of what happened. But there is then explicitly a positive passion about the way he feels now and about his intentions. He will turn Jerusalem into a place characterized by truthfulness rather than deceit, by cheerfulness rather than mourning, by gathering rather than by scattering. His relationship with the people will be restored. He knows that his promises sound implausible, but he wants people to believe them.

A Follow-Up to Zechariah from Sar-Ezer and Regem-Melek of Beth-El

To our lord Zechariah ben Berechiah:

Umm. . . . You confirmed our suspicions. But you didn't answer our original question! Should we carry on fasting and mourning?

Yahweh's words raised other worrying possibilities. What will happen if people are indeed engaged in worship and in fasting for their own sake and not really because they are serving Yahweh? What will happen if they are behaving faithlessly to one another and ignoring people like widows and orphans who have no extended family, and ordinary people who have lost their land, and migrants who never had any land? What will happen if people stop their ears now so they can't hear what the Torah tells them about such people? Will Yahweh stop his ears again? Is that another response to fasting and prayer? How definite is it that the seniors and the teenagers will hang about in the squares of Jerusalem having fun? Is Yahweh really going to bring people back from Ammon and Moab and from foreign shores to the far west?

That question makes us think of the people back in Babylon, too. Not just the Judahites—the ordinary Babylonians. When Jeremiah told our great-grandparents' generation to settle down there and make a commitment to life in Babylon, it was partly a vivid way of trying to get them used to the idea that Babylonian rule was going to keep them there for longer than they thought. But it was more than that. Jeremiah told them to pray for the Babylonians, to seek what was best for them. And what would be best for them would be to come to acknowledge that Yahweh is the true God. Is that going to happen?

From the prophet Zechariah ben Berechiah
To Sar-Ezer and Regem-Melek:

8:9"Yahweh of Armies has said this: "Your hands are to be strong, you who are listening to these words in these days from the mouth of the prophets who [were there] on the day when the house of Yahweh of Armies was founded, for building the palace. 10Because before those days there were no wages for a human being and there were no wages for an animal. For anyone going out or coming in, there was no peace from the adversary. I set all human beings one against his neighbour. 11But now I'm not acting towards the remainder of this people as in earlier days (a declaration of Yahweh of Armies), 12because the sowing will be in peace, the vine will give its fruit, the earth will give its produce, the heavens will give their dew, and I shall let the remainder of this people have all these things as a domain. 13As you became a slighting among the nations, Judah's household and Israel's household, so I shall deliver you and you will become a blessing. Don't be afraid. Your hands are to be strong."

[14]Because Yahweh of Armies has said this: "As I schemed to do something bad to you when your ancestors infuriated me (Yahweh of Armies said) and didn't relent, [15]so I have again schemed in these days to do good to Jerusalem and to Judah's household. Don't be afraid. [16]These are the things that you're to do. Speak the truth each to his neighbour. Exercise authority with truthful authority that makes for peace in your gateways. [17]Don't think up something bad in your mind each person against his neighbour. Don't love a false oath. Because all these are things to which I'm hostile (Yahweh's declaration).'"

[18]The word of Yahweh of Armies came to me. [19]"Yahweh of Armies has said this: "The fast of the fourth, the fast of the fifth, the fast of the seventh, and the fast of the tenth will become for Judah's household celebration and rejoicing, good set occasions. So love truthfulness and peace."

[20]Yahweh of Armies has said this: "Peoples and inhabitants of many towns will yet come, [21]and the inhabitants of one will go to one another saying, 'Let's go, let's go to seek Yahweh's goodwill and seek Yahweh of Armies. I myself intend to go, yes.' [22]Many peoples will come, numerous nations, to seek Yahweh of Armies in Jerusalem and to seek Yahweh's goodwill."

[23]Yahweh of Armies has said this: "In those days, when ten people from all the nations' tongues will take hold, they'll take hold of the hem of a Judahite individual's coat, saying 'We want to go with you, because we've heard that God is with you.'"' (8:9–23)

Background and Foreground

Zechariah issues the same reminder as Haggai. People had a hard time when they started returning to Jerusalem. But they gave themselves to the work, and Yahweh honored that. And the future is to be great, so keep on with the building work, continue to live faithful lives, and prove that Yahweh tells the truth. Eventually Sar-Ezer and Regem-Melek do get a response to their original question, though it's not exactly an answer. Even now, their question becomes the jumping-off ground for a promise rather than an instruction, and for another exhortation about the truthfulness and peace that need to accompany fasting. They also get an encouraging answer about what is going to happen to people like the Babylonians. They themselves don't have to do anything about it. Yahweh is going to show that he is active in their midst, and that will draw people.

A Letter to the Prophet from Jorah ben Parosh

To my lord the prophet:

My grandfather was among the Judahites who came back from Babylon and took part in the rebuilding of Jerusalem and the restoration of the temple. Our family appears in the register of the people who came back, who belong to the Jerusalem community. I am myself old enough to remember the excitement of celebrating the temple's restoration. And Yahweh gave us the impression that things were going to be great once that work was completed. But they are not, and the people in the provinces around have continued to resent the work we have done and to accuse us of things to the central authorities in Persia.

Yahweh said that the great Zerubbabel was the branch from David's tree who would sit on a throne and rule in Jerusalem, and people thought it would mean we had a king again. I know he did not quite say that, and perhaps that was wise. But Zerubbabel is dead now. So are we ever going to have a king again? Are we going to have someone who will lead us in battle so we can put down the peoples that ought to submit to Yahweh?

The related question whether and when Yahweh is really going to do something about the peoples who live near us and threaten us raises a broader one. It makes me think about the wider circle of nations around us—the Syrians to the northeast who were once part of David's empire, and the great trading nations of Tyre and Sidon to the northwest that recognized David, and the Philistines to the southwest that also eventually had to recognize him. Those were the days! Are those days ever going to come back again?

There is yet another question that in a way is even broader. Yahweh is supposed to be God of the whole world, right? His power extends to all the nations, right? And he promised to bring all Israel back to its land, right? So what about the people of Israel who are scattered all over the world? Not just away to the northeast in Babylon and Persia, but on foreign shores across the Mediterranean? When the Babylonians invaded Judah, some of our extended family, who thought there was no reason to wait for the city to fall, had the initiative to set off down to Jaffa and get on a boat from there to take them wherever it was going, so that they could find refuge somewhere and start a new life. They ended up in Ionia and we still hear from them, but it cost them everything when they had to cross the Mediterranean in that leaky boat, and there's no way they could find the money to get back. When is Yahweh going to rescue them (even if they don't want to be rescued!)?

To put it even more straight, is there any life left in the covenant that Yahweh made with Israel as a people at Sinai, when they made all those sacrificial offerings?

From the prophet
To Jorah ben Parosh:

> 9:1 Yahweh's word against the country of Hadrak,
> and Damascus its place of settling.
> Because people's eye will be towards Yahweh,
> all Israel's clans.
> 2 Hamat, too, which borders on it;
> Tyre, and Sidon because it's very smart. . . .
> 5a Ashkelon will see and be afraid,
> Gaza will writhe much,
> and Ekron, because its reliance will have
> withered. . . .
> 8 I shall camp for my house as a garrison
> against anyone passing through or
> coming back.
> No oppressor will pass through against them
> again,
> because now I shall have looked with my eyes.

> 9 Celebrate greatly, Miss Zion;
> shout, Miss Jerusalem.
> There, your king will come to you;
> he'll be faithful and one who finds
> deliverance,
> Humble and riding on a donkey,
> on an ass, the child of a she-ass.
> 10 I shall cut off chariotry from Ephraim
> and horse from Jerusalem.
> The bow of battle will be cut off;
> he will speak of peace to the nations.
> His rule will be from sea to sea,
> from the River to the ends of the earth.

[11]Yes, you [Jerusalem], by the blood of your pact:
  I'm sending off your captives.
From the pit where there's no water,
  [12]get back to the fortress, hopeful prisoners.
Yes, today I'm going to announce:
  I shall give back double to you.
[13]Because I'm directing Judah for myself as a bow,
  I'm loading Ephraim.
I shall arouse your sons, Zion,
  against your sons, Yavan [Greece], . . .
[16a]Yahweh our God will deliver them
  on that day, like a flock, his people. . . .
[17b]Grain will make the young men flourish,
  new wine the young women.
        (9:1–2, 5a, 8–13, 16a, 17b)

Background and Foreground

Yahweh declares that yes, he will put down the peoples that once submitted to David. And yes, Jerusalem will have a king again, though Yahweh doesn't say that the king will be the conqueror of those peoples. The king will ride a donkey, not a horse. Yahweh himself will do the cutting off of war machines, in both parts of Israel—both Judah and Ephraim—as well as elsewhere. The king will indeed rule over an empire with the dimensions of the one David ruled, but in doing so he will speak of peace to the nations. On the other hand, Yahweh will use Judah and Ephraim to rescue the exiles who can't otherwise get back from across the Mediterranean and bring them back to fortress Jerusalem. So they are prisoners with hope. The implication may not be that they are themselves hopeful but rather that Yahweh's promise stands over them. They will receive double blessing to make up for all the years they have been away from "home." Because yes, the covenant at Sinai, solemnized by sacrifices, still stands, and Yahweh is still committed to his people, his flock.

A Follow-Up to the Prophet from Jorah ben Parosh

To my lord the prophet:

I love those great promises, but they are so far from current reality. You know that we have to pay heavy taxes to the Persian authorities, and we therefore need decent harvests of grain and olives and grapes, in which we pay the taxes. But we haven't been having decent harvests. That disappointment doesn't compare very well with Yahweh's regular promises, let alone with the imagery in Yahweh's message to us now. The words about the king and about rescuing his people as his flock are also great promises, but they give no hint of a timeline.

We will believe that you spoke Yahweh's word and we will hold onto them. Yet they make me speak more plainly about a related matter. We have priests who offer guidance in accordance with the Torah and who encourage us to stand firm as a people in our distinctive relationship with Yahweh. We also have other priests whose guidance comes from somewhere else and who encourage us to intermarry with the peoples around, because we can afford to be open-minded and because it will be good for relationships with them. They are not worried about compromising who we are as Yahweh's people or about risking the termination of our existence as a covenant people. We have prophets who bring what I can recognize as Yahweh's message. We also have other prophets who tell us what the planets and stars allegedly reveal or what they themselves have dreamed about and who encourage people to seek contact with their loved ones who have passed, to see what they can tell them or how they can advise them.

It ought to be the job of our leaders to get a grip on these priests and prophets and diviners. But nowadays our leaders seem spineless. Their feebleness means, in effect, we have no shepherd. Or rather, what we have is unreliable shepherds, as we have unreliable priests and unreliable prophets (with respect—present company excepted). We have shepherds who are more interested in taking advantage of the sheep than in caring for them and protecting them. Either because of the lack of leaders or because of the undependability of the shepherds we do have, Yahweh's people is like a flock of sheep wandering about, not knowing where to find grass and vulnerable to wild animals. Psalm 23 says that Yahweh as shepherd has a staff to guide the sheep with and that he wields a club to protect them, but really he seems to be doing neither.

Further, not getting decent harvests means people end up having to take out loans in order to pay their taxes, which seems doubly reprehensible. And the people they have to take out loans from are these shepherds, because the people with power are also the people with money!

From the prophet
To Jorah ben Parosh:

> [10:1]Ask for rain from Yahweh
> at the time of the spring rain;
> Yahweh is the one who sends lightning flashes,
> gives them a downpour of rain,
> growth in the fields for each one.
>
> [2]Because the effigies have spoken trouble,
> the diviners have beheld falsehood.
> They speak lying dreams,
> they comfort with hollowness.
> Therefore people have strayed like a flock,

they suffer because there's no shepherd.
³Against the shepherds my anger has blazed,
    and I shall attend to the big guys.

Because Yahweh of Armies is attending to his flock,
    Judah's household.
He will make them
    like his majestic horse in battle.
⁴From it cornerstone, from it tent peg,
    from it battle bow,
From it will go out
    every overseer, together. . . .

⁶So I shall make Judah's household strong men,
    and I shall deliver Joseph's household.
I shall restore them, because I've had compassion
        on them;
    they'll be as if I had not rejected them.
Because I am Yahweh,
    their God, and I shall answer them. (10:1–4, 6)

¹³:²And on that day (a declaration of Yahweh of Armies) I shall cut off the names of the images from the country. They won't be mentioned again. Also the prophets and the defiled spirit I shall cause to pass away from the country. ³When someone prophesies again, his father and his mother, who brought him to birth, will say, "You will not live, because you've spoken falsehood in Yahweh's name." His father and his mother, who brought him to birth, will thrust him through when he prophesies.

⁴On that day the prophets will be ashamed, each one, of his vision when he prophesies. They won't wear a garment of hair so as to deceive. ⁵He will say, "I'm not

a prophet, I'm a man who works the ground, because a man acquired me from my youth." ⁶If someone says to him, "What are these wounds between your hands?" he will say, "I was wounded in my friends' house." (13:2–6)

Background and Foreground

Yahweh doesn't rise to Jorah's remark about the gap between promises and reality but simply repeats promises of good harvests and adds promises about false purveyors of guidance. Jorah's letter and Yahweh's undertakings about images and prophets reflect how the dynamics of life in Jerusalem continue as they had been in a previous era. Jeremiah 23 shows how most prophets worked with a theology and an ethic that didn't match the Torah and how they shared their dreams rather than bringing Yahweh's word. Here prophets are also secretly engaged in forms of self-harm that could somehow provoke a religious experience, like the prophets who pray to the Master (Baal) and slash themselves in the story of Elijah's confronting them in 1 Kings 18. The way most prophets function is enough to make many people simply want to dismiss the idea of prophecy or call it something else or deny being prophets.

Yahweh recognizes that the building that is Judah needs a cornerstone to hold it together. The tent that is Judah needs a tent peg to hold it secure. He will ensure it emerges.

A Follow-Up to the Prophet from Tahan ben Ammihud the Ephraimite, Scribe

To my lord the prophet:

When I heard you refer to Ephraim, the people in the north— well, at first it sounded negative, but it also implied something positive. Yahweh is going to cut off chariotry from Ephraim, but that's what he is going to do to Jerusalem as the capital of Judah, too, which implies a recognition that Ephraim still exists as a people just as much as Jerusalem and Judah do. Not everyone is prepared to think that way, especially because we have a lot of trouble with the people who live in the old area of Ephraim, the Samarians, who have got nothing to do with the real Ephraim of generations ago.

Then Yahweh was more specific. As he is going to bend the string on Judah as his bow, he said he is going to "load" Ephraim as it were, fit the bow with it as his arrow. He's going to use Ephraim alongside Judah when he rescues people from the far west. He's going to deliver Joseph's household, a wider promise that opens up the future for all ten northern clans.

And I am excited, because I am an Ephraimite. An ancestor of mine was a scribe working for the administration in Samaria in its last years as a nation. He had more clue about what was going to happen there than most people, and he was a bit better off than many people. The family story recounts how he managed to get the family together before the Assyrians were too close and get them down to Judah in a wagon before the border closed. And eventually he got a job here in Jerusalem, and he trained his sons as scribes, and they trained their sons, and so on, and I have the impression that Jerusalem became home for them. Of course, because my great-grandfather was a scribe, someone with a skill, the Babylonians took him off to Babylon, and I was born there, but they were all able to move back here when Babylon collapsed. Yet technically we are still a migrant family from Ephraim, and we don't have any land rights here. And we still haven't forgotten where we came from or what happened to our relatives who were taken off to Assyria. So my ears pricked up when you referred to Ephraim, and I want to know more about whether Yahweh is still committed to us.

From the prophet
To Tahan ben Ammihud:

10:7Ephraim will be a veritable strong man;
    their heart will rejoice as with wine.
Their children will see and rejoice;
    their heart will be joyful in Yahweh.
8I shall whistle to them and gather them,
    because I have redeemed them.
They will become many, as they were many,
    9though I sowed them among the nations.
In far-off places they will be mindful of me;
    they will live with their children and
        come back.
10I shall bring them back from the country of
        Egypt,
    collect them from Assyria.
Though I bring them to the country of Gilead and
        Lebanon,
    room won't be found for them.
11He will pass through the confining sea,
    he will strike down the sea of waves.
All the Nile's deeps will dry up,
    and the majesty of Assyria will be put down.
Egypt's club will pass away,
    12and I shall make them strong men through
        Yahweh,
    and in his name they'll go about (Yahweh's
        declaration).

11:1Open your doors, Lebanon,
    so fire can consume your cedars.
2Howl, junipers, because the cedar is falling,
    when the august are being destroyed.

Howl, Bashan oaks,
    because the fortified forest is going down.
³The sound of the shepherds' howling,
    because their eminence is destroyed.
The sound of the lions' roar,
    because Jordan's majesty is destroyed.
        (10:7–11:3)

Background and Foreground

Yahweh will indeed reestablish Ephraim as well as Judah,
the northern nation as well as the southern nation. They will so
flourish, they will need the land across the Jordan that Ephraim
lost even before the destruction of Samaria itself. Yahweh will
take action to bring back the refugees from Assyria and Egypt
and clear the land across the Jordan and in the Jordan valley
to make room for them.

A Letter to the Prophet from a Prince

To my lord the prophet:

I am a descendant of David who might therefore be involved
in shepherding Israel one day. For more than one reason, I am
apprehensive about this possibility. Yahweh has spoken to you
about the restoration of both Judah and Ephraim, and your
words remind me of his promises to Ezekiel. Yahweh has spoken
to you about bringing the scattered Israelites back from wherever
they are, and your words remind me of his promises in Isaiah.

But it's not clear that the scattered Israelites want to be gathered. Jorah's descendants are quite happy in Ionia. Judahites
in the cities at the heart of the Persian Empire are quite happy
there. They were born there. Jerusalem—to them it's just a far-
off, primitive, run-down place out on the skirts of the empire.

And the people who do live here in Jerusalem, the people who never left and the people who returned from the areas around and the people like my family who did want to come back from Babylon: they don't mind listening to those diviners and dreamers you talked about. They like consulting the effigies of the grandparents who have passed and asking them about what they should do.

It scares me because I'm not clear that Yahweh will continue tolerating these people, any more than he did in Ezekiel's day. Ezekiel had a neat picture of Judah and Ephraim as two sticks that Yahweh would join together and make into one stick, which is what they were supposed to be. Maybe he will now break it instead. He said he would make a covenant with them that would mean life going really well under the shepherding of the Davidic prince, but maybe he will cancel the covenant. You yourself have spoken of Yahweh putting down people like the Philistines, but maybe he will use them to bring calamity on us as they did before. Maybe we will end up with an alternative self-indulgent shepherd, of the kind Ezekiel also knew in his day, a shepherd who will actually serve other gods, even if he doesn't recognize that this is what he doing.

From the prophet
To the prince:

> 11:4Yahweh my God said this: 'Tend the flock to be killed, 5whose acquirers will kill them and won't be liable, whose sellers will say, "Yahweh be blessed! I shall be rich," and whose shepherds won't have pity on them. 6Because I shall no more have pity on the country's inhabitants (Yahweh's declaration). There, I'm going to make people vulnerable, each to his neighbour's hand and to his king's hand. They will crush the country, and I shall not rescue it from their hand.'

⁷So I pastured the sheep to be killed, therefore the lowliest of the flock. I got myself two staffs, I called one 'Beauty,' and the other I called 'Binders,' and I pastured the sheep. ⁸I disposed of three shepherds in one month. With my whole being I lost patience with them, and with their whole being they loathed me, too. ⁹So I said, 'I shall not pasture you. The one who dies may die and the one who gets disposed of may get disposed of, and the ones who remain, each may eat the flesh of her neighbour.'

¹⁰I got my staff 'Beauty' and broke it, contravening my pact that I had solemnized with all the peoples. ¹¹So it was contravened on that day, and the lowliest of the sheep, who were keeping watch towards me, thus acknowledged that it was Yahweh's word. ¹²I said to them, 'If it's good in your eyes, give me my pay; it not, withhold it.' They weighed out my pay, thirty silver pieces. ¹³Yahweh said to me, 'Throw it to the potter' (the worthy magnificence that I was worth to them). So I took the thirty silver pieces and threw them to the potter in Yahweh's house. ¹⁴And I broke my second staff, 'Binders,' to contravene the brotherhood between Judah and Israel.

¹⁵Yahweh said to me again, 'Get yourself the implements of a stupid shepherd. ¹⁶Because here I am, I'm going to raise up a shepherd in the country who won't attend to the ones who are disposed of or seek the young one or heal the injured or sustain the one who stands firm, but will eat the flesh of the fat one and tear off their hoofs.

¹⁷Hey, non-entity shepherds,
    abandoning the flock:
A sword on your arm

and on your right eye!
May his arm quite wither,
    his right eye go quite blind!' (11:4–17)

13:7Sword, rouse yourself against my shepherd,
    against a man who is my envoy (a declaration
      of Yahweh of Armies).
Strike down my shepherd, the flock is to scatter;
    I shall turn back my hand against the
      little ones.
8In all the country (Yahweh's declaration)
    two parts in it will be cut off, will perish.
A third will be left in it.
    9but I shall bring the third into the fire.
I shall smelt them as one smelts silver,
    test them as one tests gold.
It will call in my name,
    and I myself shall answer it,
I shall have said, "It is my people,"
    and it will say, "Yahweh is my God." (13:7–9)

Background and Foreground

The prophet is to act as if he were a shepherd. In effect, Zerubbabel had been Judah's shepherd, and you could describe any subsequent governor as its shepherd. As far as we know, no Davidic prince governed Judah after Zerubbabel's day, and we don't know who the actual shepherd-governor now is. In his vision or story or drama, the prophet looks after the flock with his two staffs and gets rid of three other shepherds (presumably rogue shepherds). But events confirm the prince's assessment of the flock, and the prophet/shepherd therefore disposes of the mangy sheep for a sum that is hardly worth keeping.

In passing on this report of his commission, he is speaking not merely for the sake of the prince. As usual, a message from

Yahweh is reported for the sake of all the people. Maybe if they overhear this commission, it will shake them to their senses. It wouldn't be surprising if some of the governors serving the Persian king were faithful to Yahweh and to the Judahite people, and others were not. The latter kind would be rogue shepherds. When Yahweh gives the prophet the second commission, to embody the work of a rogue shepherd, it is even more obvious that he is reporting it for the sake of the people, though also perhaps for the sake of an actual rogue shepherd, in the hope that he may heed Yahweh's threat. Otherwise, the flock will end up decimated, though such threats by Yahweh regularly presuppose that the devastation will not be the end.

A Follow-Up to the Prophet from a Prince

To my lord the prophet:

You have heard of the terrible stabbing in Jerusalem. We are not a city characterized by random violence. There have been occasions when robbers have stabbed someone, or when someone has stabbed a robber, or when a betrayed husband has stabbed his wife's lover. And in the distant past there have been occasions when prophets were set upon and when kings were assassinated. But that seems to belong to another place or another time.

It makes me ask about the future of Jerusalem. There are such promises of peace and happiness attached to the city. They include your own promises. People will sit under their vine and fig tree and live in harmony and faithfulness with one another. Is Yahweh really committed to Jerusalem, still? Do we have the strength to buttress its future? Is Yahweh still committed to cleansing us from the stain of an event like this one?

And what about the city's other form of vulnerability? We

are still periodically under pressure from the other peoples around. What if they combine together and attack us? What if their aim is to eliminate the city's leadership that goes back to David and Levi? Will the Davidic circle be strong enough to stand firm? What if they overcome the area of Judah around us that has no fortifications and then blockade Jerusalem from that base?

From the prophet
To the prince:

> 12:1b A declaration of Yahweh,
>   the one who stretched out the heavens,
> Who founded the earth,
>   who shaped the spirit of humanity within it.

2"There, I'm going to make Jerusalem a chalice that causes reeling to all the peoples around. It will also be against Judah during the siege against Jerusalem.

3On that day, I shall make Jerusalem a stone hard to lift for all the peoples. All who lift it will seriously injure themselves when all the nations of the earth gather against it.

4On that day (Yahweh's declaration), I shall strike down every horse with panic and its rider with madness. Over Judah's household I shall open my eyes, but every horse belonging to the peoples I shall strike with blindness. 5Judah's clans will say to themselves, "Jerusalem's inhabitants are my strength, through Yahweh of Armies, their God."

6On that day, I shall make Judah's clans like a firepot among trees, like a fiery torch among sheaves. They will consume all the peoples around, to the right and the left. And Jerusalem will again live in its place, in

Jerusalem. [7]Yahweh will deliver Judah's tents first, so that the glory of David's household and the glory of Jerusalem's population will not be greater than Judah.'

[8]On that day Yahweh will shield over Jerusalem's population. Someone among them who is liable to collapse will be like David on that day, and David's household will be like gods, like Yahweh's envoy going before them.

[9]On that day I shall seek to annihilate all the nations that come against Jerusalem, [10]but I shall pour out on David's household and on Jerusalem's population a spirit of grace and of prayers for grace. They will look to me concerning someone they've thrust through, and they will lament over him with the lamentation for an only son, and express distress for him like the distress over a firstborn.

[11]On that day the lamentation in Jerusalem will be great, like the lamentation for Hadad-rimmon in Megiddo Valley. [12a]The country will lament, kin-group by kin-group by itself. . . . [13:1]On that day there will be a fountain opened for David's household and Jerusalem's inhabitants, for purification and for cleansing. (12:1–13:1)

Background and Foreground

Yahweh offers four reassurances to the prince. First, Yahweh's power undergirds and guarantees Jerusalem's future. Second, Yahweh is therefore not going to let Jerusalem be overwhelmed, even by people who have already gotten control of much of Judah; on the contrary, their designs on Jerusalem will be the cause of their own downfall. In Persian times much of "Judah" was outside the province of Judah, and much of it was occupied by the Edomites. Third, Yahweh will inspire Jerusalem into prayers for grace and into mourning (we don't know who the person is who has been stabbed, or what the lamentation for Hadad-Rimmon was). And fourth, Yahweh will provide for the city's cleansing.

A Final Follow-Up to the Prophet from the Prince

To my lord the prophet:

Some of us have been working hard here at the priorities that concern you. We have been trying to get a grip on the way the finances work so that we can make the payments to the Persian capital in a fashion that reduces the burden on ordinary people. We have been trying to negotiate more friendly relationships with the peoples around, though we're not making much progress. We haven't been able to do anything about the city's defenses, and that insecurity is the thing that most keeps me awake at night. I have been working with the senior priest to try to get some oversight of the priests and to improve standards of religious education so that we can wean people off the traditional practices that they are always inclined to fall back on. But I confess I get tired. And it's easy for me to lose sight of the big picture and of what Yahweh promises. Is there a vision you can offer me?

From the prophet
To the prince:

> 14:1There, a Day of Yahweh is coming, and your spoil [Jerusalem] will be shared out within you. 2I shall gather all the nations to Jerusalem for battle. The town will be captured, the houses will be plundered, the women will be ravished and half the town will go out into exile.

But the rest of the people will not be cut off from the town, ³and Yahweh will go out and do battle against those nations, as he does battle on a day of engagement.

⁴On that day his feet will stand on the Mount of Olives which faces Jerusalem to the east. The Mount of Olives will split in half from east to west, a very big ravine; half of the mountain will move away northward, half of it southward. ⁵You people will flee by the ravine between my mountains, because the ravine between the mountains will reach to Azal. You will flee as you fled from before the earthquake in the days of Uzziah king of Judah. But Yahweh my God will come—all the sacred ones will be with you.

⁶On that day there won't be light from the glorious ones; they will dwindle. ⁷There'll be one day (it is known to Yahweh), not day and not night; at evening time it will be light.

⁸On that day living water will go out from Jerusalem, half of it to the eastern sea, half of it to the western sea. It will happen in summer and in winter. ⁹Yahweh will be king over all the earth.

On that day Yahweh will be one and his name one. ¹⁰The entire country will turn round [and be] like the steppe, from Geba to Rimmon south of Jerusalem, but it [Jerusalem] will rise up and stay in its place, from the Benjamin Gate to the place of the First Gate, to the Corner Gate, and from Hananel's Tower to the king's winepresses. ¹¹People will live in it, and devoting will not happen anymore. Jerusalem will live in confidence.

¹²But this will be the epidemic that Yahweh will impose on all the peoples that made war against Jerusalem: making someone's flesh waste away while he stands on his feet, his eyes waste away in their sockets, and his tongue waste away in their mouth.

[13]On that day a great panic from Yahweh will come upon them. They'll take hold, each person, of his neighbour's hand, and his hand will rise against his neighbour's hand. [14]Judah, too, will do battle at Jerusalem. The resources of all the nations around will be gathered—gold and silver and clothing, a great quantity.

[15]Like this epidemic, so will be the epidemic affecting horse, mule, camel, donkey, and every animal that will be in those camps. [16]But everyone who is left from all the nations that come against Jerusalem will go up year by year to bow low to the King, Yahweh of Armies, and to observe the Sukkot Festival. [17]Whichever does not go up from the kin-groups of the earth to Jerusalem to bow low to the King, Yahweh of Armies, there'll be no rain on them. [18]If Egypt's kin-group doesn't go up and doesn't come, there'll be none on them; there'll be the epidemic that Yahweh imposes on the nations that don't go up to observe the Sukkot Festival. [19]This will be [the penalty for] the wrongdoing of Egypt and the wrongdoing of all the nations that don't go up to observe the Sukkot Festival. [20]On that day, upon a horse's bells will be 'Sacred to Yahweh.' The pots in Yahweh's house will be like the basins before the altar. [21]Every pot in Jerusalem and Judah will be sacred to Yahweh of Armies. All the people who offer sacrifice will come and take some of them and cook in them. There'll be no more trader in the house of Yahweh of Armies on that day. (14:1–21)

Background and Foreground

In the visions he presents, Yahweh has no promise that the city's future is going to be disaster free. Indeed, there will be disaster as horrifying as the one brought by the Babylonians.

He does again promise that disaster will not be the end and that he will provide some of its people with a miraculous way of escape from being overwhelmed (we don't know where Azal was). He and his heavenly entourage will be there, light and water will be miraculously plentiful, Jerusalem will be exalted over the whole land. There will be no more "devoting" (the word suggests offering people to Yahweh, which in this kind of connection means killing them). For the nations, too, Yahweh has an equivalent combination of grimness and promise. They too will thus join in the worship of the sacred city, which will transform the beasts of war, the vessels of everyday life, and the occupations of business.

LETTERS TO
MALACHI

Like the people in the time of Haggai and Zechariah and the time of Ezra and Nehemiah, the people in Malachi's day have a "governor" (1:8) overseeing them. It is a concrete indication that Malachi, too, belongs in the Persian era and that the order of the Twelve Scrolls puts Malachi in a plausible place among the Twelve Prophets, at the end.

A Letter to Malachi from Hadassah
bat Pedaiah of the clan of Simeon

To my lord Malachi in Jerusalem:

A while ago now my great-grandmother Judith bat Jachin wrote to your colleague Obadiah about the way the Edomites were occupying more and more of our land in the Negeb, and Obadiah related to us a promise from Yahweh that the situation would be reversed. Over the years, our family has treasured Obadiah's reply. We treasured it because of what it was: to think that we had a letter with a message from Yahweh! We also treasured it because of what it actually said. But the opposite to what it promised is what has been happening ever since. The Edomites are occupying more and more of the land. My family has had to move north to an area near Beth-Lehem, to some land that Judahites abandoned at the time of the Babylonian invasion. We live okay as squatters, but it doesn't exactly suggest Yahweh being loyal to us and caring for us in the way the Torah promises.

From the prophet Malachi
To Hadassah bat Pedaiah of the clan of Simeon:

> [1:2]'I've been loyal to you,' Yahweh said. But you say, 'How have you been loyal to us?' 'Esau was Jacob's brother, wasn't he (Yahweh's declaration)? But I was loyal to Jacob [3]and I was hostile to Esau. I'm making his mountains a desolation, his domain to belong to wilderness jackals.' [4]Because Edom says, 'We've been crushed, but we'll build the wastes again,' Yahweh of Armies has said this: 'Those people may build, but I myself will tear down.' They will be called 'Faithless Territory' and 'the people Yahweh has condemned permanently.' [5]Your own eyes will see it. You yourselves will say, 'Yahweh is great, beyond Israel's territory.' (1:2–5)

Background and Foreground

Yahweh urges Hadassah to remember the facts of her ancestors' past from a long time back, and on that basis he urges her to believe that he is acting to put Edom down now and to restore Israel's territory to it, even though there's nothing to be seen yet.

A Letter to Malachi from Sheal
ben Telem, the Levite

To my lord Malachi:

As a Levite, I am actively engaged with what goes on in the temple. I don't take part in actually offering the sacrifices, splattering the blood, and so on, but I am involved in helping the people who bring sacrifices and in preparing things and cleaning up afterwards and sorting things out if they go wrong. I open the doors first thing in the morning and rekindle the fire on the altar. I feed the fire through the day and close down the sanctuary after the evening offering. So we Levites who aren't priests in the strict sense are close to the priests in their work, and we hear them talking to one another before and after the services. And I'm troubled about the way they talk. It's as if they've forgotten the seriousness of what they are doing and the importance of it and the privilege of what we are all occupied with. I guess it's an inevitable temptation for anyone who is professionally engaged in religious activities.

Anyway, the priests have also gotten lax in the quality of the animals they are prepared to offer for the sacrifices. When someone brings a sheep that's lame, they tell the person, "It's okay, it doesn't matter, it's still a sheep." They especially take that attitude if the person is someone important, who actually ought to be more able to give something of good quality. The priests don't see themselves as insulting Yahweh, but really that's what they're doing. They've given up on the idea that only the best is good enough for Yahweh.

Now the covenant that Yahweh made with our ancestor Levi applies to me as well as to the actual priests, and I wonder whether they are imperiling our clan's position for all of us. I wonder whether Yahweh will stop working through the blessings that the priests pronounce on us all when they say, "Yahweh bless you and keep you, Yahweh make his face shine on you and show favor to you, Yahweh lift up his face upon you and give you well-being." What do you think?

From the prophet Malachi
To Sheal ben Telem, Levite:

1:6 "A son honours his father, a servant his lord. If I'm a father, where's the honour for me? If I'm a Lord, where's the awe for me?" Yahweh of Armies said to you, priests who disdain my name. You say, "How have we disdained your name?" 7You're presenting defiled food on my altar. You say, "How have we defiled you?" By your saying, "Yahweh's table can be disdained." 8When you bring up something blind for sacrifice, there's nothing bad. When you bring up something lame or sick, there's nothing bad. Present it to your governor, please. Will he accept you? Will he have regard to you? (Yahweh of Armies has said.)' 9Now, please seek Yahweh's goodwill so that he shows favour to us. This has come from your hand. Will he have regard to any of you? (Yahweh of Armies has said.)

10'Who indeed is there among you who'll shut the doors, and not light a fire on my altar to no end! I find no delight in you (Yahweh of Armies has said) and I shall not accept an offering from your hand.

11Because from the sun's rising to its setting my name is great among the nations and in every place incense is offered to my name, and a pure offering, because my name is great among the nations (Yahweh of Armies has said). 12But you're treating it as ordinary when you say, "The Lord's table is defiled, and its fruit, its food, can be disdained," [13]or say, "This is a wea-riness," and blow it off (Yahweh of Armies has said), or bring something stolen or lame or sick, and bring it as the offering. Should I accept it from your hand? (Yahweh has said.) [14]Cursed is the cheat when there's a male in his flock but he pledges and sacrifices to the Lord something devastated. Because I am a great king (Yahweh of Armies has said) and my name is held in awe among the nations.

[2:1]So now to you priests, this order. [2]If you don't lis-ten and don't receive it into your mind to give honour to my name (Yahweh of Armies has said), I shall send off a curse among you. I shall curse your blessings. Indeed, I have cursed it, because you don't receive it into your mind. [3]Here am I, I'm going to reprimand your seed. I'm going to spread faeces on your faces, the faeces from your festival sacrifice. Someone will carry you out to it. [4]And you will acknowledge that I have sent off this order to you so that my pact with Levi might exist (Yahweh of Armies has said). [5]My pact with him was life and well-being, and I gave them to him, with awe. He was in awe of me. He was in dread of my name.

[6]True instruction was in his mouth;
    evil wasn't found on his lips.
In well-being and in uprightness he walked
        with me,
    and he turned many back from waywardness.
[7]Because a priest's lips keep watch on knowledge;
    people seek instruction from his mouth,
    because he is an envoy of Yahweh of Armies.

[8]But you've turned aside from the way. You've made many people collapse through your instruction. You've

devastated Levi's pact (Yahweh of Armies has said). ⁹I myself in turn am making you shameful and low to the entire people, on account of the fact that you don't keep watch on my ways but you show regard in the instruction.' (1:6–2:9)

Background and Foreground

Through much of the Middle Eastern and Mediterranean world, there were Judahites who had not come back to Israel when they had the chance, but they were making offerings where they lived, and Yahweh's shocking affirmation is that their offerings, which would fall short of the sacrifices the priests offered in the temple in Jerusalem, actually brought more glory to Yahweh. Sheal does have something to worry about.

A Letter to Malachi from Naomi bat Jehoiada

To my lord Malachi:

I write to you because I have nowhere else to turn. My husband Jonathan ben Elnathan, a priest, has thrown me out of the house. I am nearly forty and I have been unable to get pregnant. We've tried and tried but it's never happened. I have my monthly periods, so it ought to happen, but it hasn't. Well, it has happened. When I was in my twenties, I seemed to have gotten pregnant twice, but then I lost the baby both times. Finally, my husband did what lots of men in that position do—he got another wife so he could have a baby with her. It was a painful thing for me, but I couldn't really complain. I recognized that we will need someone to look after us when we get older.

So he hired a girl from her parents who would help with the

house and with the work and then they would be married, and she was okay with the arrangement. Of course, the fact that she was an attractive youngster was hard for me. But what I really couldn't cope with was that she was a Moabite. One of her ancestors had fought here during the Babylonian campaign in Judah, and he had liked it here and had moved the family here after the fall of Jerusalem when the Babylonians encouraged that. It might not have been so bad if they had properly assimilated, but they have carried on meeting with other Moabites and praying to Chemosh, the Moabite god. And Jonathan is a priest, and he lets it happen!

So his relationship with her became a huge issue between us and we used to argue about it, and eventually she did get pregnant and she had her baby, and she started acting superior. We argued some more and then eventually he said he was fed up with it and he was simply throwing me out and I could go and live with my brother and his wife.

Is he allowed to do that?

From the prophet Malachi
To Naomi bat Jehoiada:

2:10We all of us have one Father, don't we? One God created us, didn't he? Why do we break faith, each with his brother, in treating our ancestors' pact as ordinary? 11Judah has broken faith. An offence has been committed in Israel and in Jerusalem, because Judah has treated as ordinary what is sacred to Yahweh, to which he is loyal, and has married the daughter of a strange god. 12May Yahweh cut off the person who does this (anyone who arises and anyone who responds) from Jacob's tents, even one who presents an offering to Yahweh of Armies.

13And you do this second thing, covering Yahweh's altar with tears, crying and wailing because he's no

longer regarding the offering or receiving it with acceptance from your hand, [14]and you've said, 'On account of
what?' On account of the fact that Yahweh is a witness
between you and the wife of your youth, with whom
you've broken faith, when she was your partner and
your covenanted woman. [15]Didn't One make us, and
isn't the remainder of spirit his? And what is the One
seeking? Godly offspring. So you will guard yourself
in your spirit. Someone is not to break faith with the
wife of your youth. [16]When he's hostile so as to divorce
(Yahweh the God of Israel has said), he makes violence
a cover over his clothing (Yahweh of Armies has said).
So you're to keep watch for yourself in your spirit and
not break faith. (2:10–16)

Background and Foreground

The short answer, then, is, "No, he's not." Several principles are involved. As well as being husband and wife, these
two people are brother and sister within Yahweh's family;
that's one reason. The sacredness of Israel is another. The fact
that Jonathan made a promise is another. For Jonathan and
Naomi, of course, there's an irony and a further grief in the
fact that they would have loved to have the chance to bring up
godly offspring. Life is complicated.

A Follow-Up to Malachi from
Naomi bat Jehoiada

To my lord Malachi:

I'm grateful for your support, but it looks as if it's not going
to make any difference. It's not going to make Jonathan have
me back. Actually, I wouldn't want to go back now. And your

argument is not likely to make him support me. He can claim that he has a wife and baby to support and that I will be okay with my brother's family.

But it leaves me disgruntled. I've been faithful to Yahweh all my life. I made sure that we paid our tithes. We kept the Sabbath. So many times I went to the temple with little offerings, to accompany my prayers that I would be able to get pregnant, but it didn't work. And I know women who were supposedly committed to Yahweh and were also secretly consulting someone who had passed, their grandmother maybe, or even making secret offerings to other gods, and they kept having babies. Yahweh just doesn't seem fair.

From the prophet Malachi
To Naomi bat Jehoiada:

2:17You've wearied Yahweh with your words. You've said, 'How have we wearied him?' When you say, 'Everyone who does something bad is good in Yahweh's eyes. In them he takes delight.' Or 'Where is the God who exercises authority?'
3:1a'Here am I, I'm going to send my envoy, and he'll clear the way before me.' Suddenly there will come to his palace the Lord for whom you are looking.
3:1bSo the envoy of the pact whom you want—there, he's coming (Yahweh of Armies has said). 2But who's going to endure the day of his coming? Who's going to stand when he appears? Because he'll be like a smelter's fire or like launderer's soap. 3He'll sit smelting and purifying silver. He'll purify the Levites and refine them like gold and silver, and they'll be Yahweh's, people who take up an offering in faithfulness. 4The offering of Judah and Jerusalem will please Yahweh as in the days gone by, in former years. (2:17–3:4)

Background and Foreground

Naomi didn't say "everyone," but it's tempting to make one's own experience the only fact that counts. But one response when life doesn't turn out the way the Torah and Proverbs promise is to remind oneself that they implicitly offer generalizations rather than universals. Another response is the one from which Malachi began: the history of what God has done gives us key clues to the real truth. But the response that Yahweh offers here is that Yahweh intends to make things work out for his people. It's a warning for Jonathan or (in a strange way) a promise to Naomi, that as a member of the priesthood, he will get "smelted" (3:3).

Another Letter to Malachi from Sheal ben Telem, the Levite

To my lord Malachi:

There's something else I see as a Levite. It affects us all as Levites, and it affects the priests, but it also affects needy people in the city. The community are not good about bringing their tithes. The way the system is supposed to work is that they bring a tenth of their produce, one in ten of the lambs that are born to their sheep, one in ten of the pots they make, and so on—or an equivalent amount of silver. But people are lax about it. In a way, you can't blame them. These are tough times, and sometimes the harvest doesn't come out very well, and people have to pay taxes to the administration as well as the tithes, partly because the administration has to send taxes to the Persian capital in Susa.

But one point about tithes is that they go to provide for people who can't grow their own food or breed their own sheep because they don't have land. So serious consequences follow from a shortfall in tithes. Obviously, I feel it for myself, because it's true of me as a Levite, engaged in ministry. But I also feel it for other people who can't grow their own food or breed their own animals. That includes the sort of people who have come to live here because they had to leave their own country (maybe they are runaway slaves). It includes widows and orphans if they have lost control of the family land and haven't been adopted into a family. No tithes, they starve.

From the prophet Malachi
To Sheal ben Telem, Levite:

> 3:6Because I am Yahweh, I haven't changed, and you're Jacob's descendants, you haven't come to an end. 7Given that from your ancestors' days you've turned aside from my laws and not kept them: come back to me and I'll come back to you (Yahweh of Armies has said).
>
> You'll say, "How shall we come back?" 8Does a person cheat God? Because you're cheating me. You'll say, "How have we cheated you?" In tithe and contribution. 9You're subjected to a curse, and you're cheating me—the nation, all of it. 10Bring the entire tithe into the storehouse, so that there may be food in my house, and test me by this, please (Yahweh of Armies has said), if I don't open the heavens' floodgates and empty out blessing on you until there's no need. 11I'll reprimand the devourer for you, and it won't destroy the fruit of the ground for you, and the vine in the open country won't miscarry for you (Yahweh of Armies has said). 12All the nations will count you fortunate, because you'll be a delightful land (Yahweh of Armies has said). (3:6–12)

Background and Foreground

As the collection of Malachi's little messages draws near its end, Yahweh's declaration is reminiscent of the one at the beginning, about his commitment to "Jacob." They had said that he didn't look like someone committed to them; now in the full and free exchange of views that characterizes these messages, Yahweh returns the compliment. There are two aspects to the significance of tithes, or perhaps three. Tithes are a way Israelites support the ministry in the temple. They are a way they care for needy people who don't have their own land on which to grow things or to raise animals. And they are an expression of people's recognition of God as the giver of all that they have. The pressure on the Israelites means they are failing in all directions. Yahweh's challenge is to give in the conviction that they will then receive.

A Letter to Malachi from Shemaiah ben Elnathan, Scribe

To my lord Malachi:

I am scribe for a commemorative document that is kept by people who returned from Babylon and are so grateful to Yahweh for the fact that we were able to return. There are various things about the record. It means our names are down there in writing, with the names of our families, and we keep it up to date with a record of when someone dies and when a baby is born. We include in it events like a marvelous healing or other answer to prayer.

I am writing because we wondered whether it might be any use to other people. We know there are people who are discouraged about serving Yahweh. We've heard them speaking strong words about it. They think that serving Yahweh is pointless and that they would be better off not bothering. And they have thereby tempted Yahweh to punish them, but they have gotten away with it. It makes us sad, and we wonder how they can be drawn back to Yahweh, and whether our scroll might help.

From the prophet Malachi
To Shemaiah ben Elnathan:

3:13'You've made your words strong against me (Yahweh has said). You'll say, "What have we spoken to ourselves against you?" 14You've said, "Serving God is empty in results. What was the gain when we kept his charge and walked in gloom before Yahweh of Armies? 15So now we count the arrogant fortunate. The people who act in faithlessness have both been built up and have also tested God and escaped.'

16Then the people who were in awe of Yahweh talked, each with his neighbour, and Yahweh heeded and listened, and a remembrance scroll was written before him regarding the people who were in awe of Yahweh and who esteemed his name. 17'For me they will be a special possession (Yahweh of Armies has said) for the day that I'm preparing. I shall have pity on them as someone has pity on his son who serves him. 18You'll again see the difference between the faithful and the faithless, between the one who serves God over against the one who has not served him.

4:1Because there—the day is coming, burning like an oven, when all the arrogant and all the people who act in faithlessness will be stubble, and the day that's coming will burn them up (Yahweh of Armies has said) so that it doesn't leave them root or branch. 2But there will rise for you who are in awe of my name a faithful sun with healing in its rays. You'll go out and jump like well-fed bullocks. ³You'll trample the faithless, because they'll be ashes under the soles of your feet, on that day that I'm making (Yahweh of Armies has said).

⁴Be mindful of Moses my servant's instruction, which I ordered him for all Israel at Horeb, laws and rulings. ⁵There, I'm sending you Elijah the prophet before the coming of the great and awe-inspiring Day of Yahweh. ⁶He will turn back the mind of parents to children and the mind of children to parents, so that I don't come and strike down the country with "devoting."' (3:13–4:6)

Background and Foreground

I don't know whether or not that scroll might be useful to the people who are feeling discouraged. After all, what does help such people? But Yahweh does comment on how much the scroll pleases him. And their being the people they are will stand them in good stead on the day when Yahweh acts.

Whether or not their scroll does anything for the discouraged, Elijah's ministry will be restorative for them. But solemnly, then, the last word in the Twelve Prophets (and thus the last word in the First Testament) is that word "devoting," the word for offering people to Yahweh that in this kind of connection means killing them, as if they were a sacrifice. The last chapter of Zechariah had promised a day when there will be no more of it, but Malachi doesn't want people to relax too easily. When Jews read the Scriptures, they repeat the previous promise: "There, I'm sending you Elijah the prophet before the coming of the great and awe-inspiring Day of Yahweh." If people heed his message, then there won't need to be any more of that devoting.

And if you are reading the First Testament in the context of the New Testament, then it's only a few pages later when someone who looks like Elijah appears (see Matthew 3).

A FINAL LETTER TO
THE PROPHETS

The more one reads your promises, the more exotic they become. I wonder what you really thought of them yourselves, how you thought of the future, and how we should think of it?

Maybe we can approach that question by considering your threats as well as your promises, and your analyses of the present as well as your projections about the future. You were consistently over the top, though the same is true of Isaiah, Jeremiah, and Ezekiel. You overstated the nature of people's waywardness and you overdramatized it. You did the same with Yahweh's intentions, whether you were relaying threats or promises. Such hyperbole makes some readers take no notice; they prefer statements that are fact-checkable. It makes other readers take notice. It looks as if the influencers and opinion formers in the Jewish community were the second kind of reader. They were persuaded both that Yahweh really did speak to you and that the community should hold onto these messages. And Jesus and the New Testament writers agreed with them.

Both the analyses and the threats were overstatements, but they were overstatements of something that was real, not a fantasizing about something that was unreal. The Assyrians did overrun Samaria. The Babylonians did conquer Jerusalem.

Something parallel applies to your promises. You did enable Judahites to return from Babylon and restore the temple and get a Davidic prince appointed governor of Jerusalem. As the calamity was not as big a calamity as you said, the renewal was not as magnificent a renewal as you said; but they were not nothing.

Both the action and the shortfall were significant manifestations of who Yahweh is. It's more obvious with the calamity. It was morally (and perhaps theologically) necessary for Yahweh to discipline your people; it reflected something of who he is. But it was also theologically (and perhaps morally) necessary for Yahweh not to destroy them; it reflected something of who he is. Likewise, it was theologically (and perhaps morally) necessary for Yahweh to restore your people; it also reflected something of who he is.

In speaking of calamity or restoration, one could say you were speaking of Yahweh's Day, whether or not you actually used that phrase. And what actually happened in fulfillment of your threats and promises was indeed *a* Day of Yahweh if not *the* Day of Yahweh. It was a partial embodiment at a particular moment of a complete embodiment that will come one day. You invite us to live in light of the kind of portrait you give, which can prepare us for *a* Day of Yahweh. It can also prepare us for *the* Day of Yahweh.

INDEX OF PASSAGES FROM
THE TWELVE PROPHETS

WORD BIBLICAL COMMENTARY
Daniel
John Goldingay

The Word Biblical Commentary delivers the best in biblical scholarship from the leading scholars of our day. This series emphasizes a thorough analysis of textual, linguistic, structural, and theological evidence. The result is judicious and balanced insight into the meanings of the text in the framework of biblical theology.

WORD BIBLICAL THEMES
Daniel

John Goldingay

A companion to the acclaimed Word
Biblical Commentary, the Word Biblical
Themes series helps readers discover
the most important themes of a book
of the Bible. This series distills the
theological essence of a given book

of Scripture and serves it up in ways that enrich the preaching,
teaching, worship, and discipleship of God's people.